# Book Description

Discover how baby boomers like you can get their portfolios booming with crypto, even with zero experience.

Are you looking to make money online with crypto?

This method seems to be the ideal strategy to earn passive income, but all the moving parts make it easy to feel overwhelmed.

It also seems as though the whole process is time-consuming and takes a lot of knowledge to be lucrative.

If these are some of the concerns you have, you're in the right place and should keep reading.

Cryptocurrencies are evolving by the day, and more people are profiting from it while you're stuck figuring out how they're doing it.

It can be frustrating, but the good news is that with the right action-based guide and mindset, you'll soon be on the path to achieving your financial goals.

C.B. McGee has all the answers you're looking for, and you'll benefit from his methods especially if you're someone who:

Thinks cryptocurrencies are too expensive

Wants to know what all the hype is about

Worried about how to protect your investments

Doesn't want to regret not investing in this potentially life-changing opportunity

The first step to becoming successful in the world of crypto is having the insight and understanding that other wealthy investors have—and using it to take constructive action.

In *The Baby Boomer's Guide to Cryptocurrency*, here is just a fraction of what you will discover:

A comprehensive guide to the world of cryptocurrencies so you can keep up with all the latest trends

How people are making millions of dollars from crypto that started as a joke

The most powerful investment strategies so you can always get the most bang for your buck

The latest research in crypto mining and how to know if it is worth investing your time and money

A goldmine of crypto terminology that's easy to understand and even teach to others

Professional secrets on buying, selling, and investing crypto, so it is safe and profitable

The underground playbook of how to determine if a new coin will be the next Bitcoin

And much more.

From abstract concepts to the most technical details, this highly informative, action-based guide will reveal everything you need to get started on earning your first dollar with crypto.

Are you ready to become the crypto investor that your friends and family ask for advice?

It is time to start taking advantage of crypto before it is too late. The best way to start is by scrolling up and clicking the "Add to Cart" button now.

# The Baby Boomer's Guide to Cryptocurrency

## How to Buy, Sell, Trade, Mine, and Make Cryptocurrency Part of your Portfolio

C.B McGee

# Table of Contents

Contents

I was fortunate in building a business that allowed me to retire at 50 years of age, but I realize that most people do not have that luxury. Cryptocurrency is one of the ways that I have used to make money in retirement. I have been able to pay for 3 houses with Crypto profits!

As a gift to you for buying this book, I would like to give you a copy of my E-book, 12 Ways to Create an Online Income, because everyone can always use a few extra bucks!

Go to www.cbmcgee.com to get your free copy.

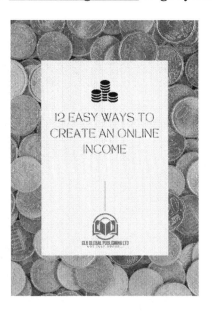

# Introduction

By opening this guide, you're demonstrating a willingness to understand a market that is predicted to grow exponentially in the next few years. By using great insight into cryptocurrency, from first-hand experience and research that others have been following since its inception, you will be accessing a simplified guide on the incredible subject known as *online trade*.

Despite the controversy, cryptocurrency (or crypto, for short) has risen from its previous valuations, and many investing options have recently reached their all-time high. Many once believed that Bitcoin was a cash-grab when it was worth nearly pennies to a dollar, yet today, those people use their shares to buy houses and set themselves up for retirement.

It truly is an exciting time to be an investor, but it can just as easily be overwhelming, especially if you are new to online trade. The numbers can be incredibly confusing, and the volatility of the market is enough to scare anyone away from this profitable landscape.

This guide will serve as a crash course on crypto so that you can invest with a clear understanding of how the online trade works. The goal of any investment is to come out with a return, and the daily trading of crypto has the potential to do just that.

What's interesting about digital money is how it is available. Given its online stage and the always developing condition of the internet, individuals located anywhere can contribute and sell at any time. Be that as it may, without legitimate information about or a foundation for how the exchange functions, it is unimaginably simple to rapidly lose your underlying venture.

Individuals have lost mind-boggling amounts of cash within minutes due to careless mistakes. Additionally, the mistakes investors make are common and could have been avoided had they obtained the information required to do so.

A significant takeaway from this guide is the amount of data you will acquire, as each page is loaded with significant exploration points consolidated in a simplified manner.

The information contained in this guide was compiled from my own experience, as well as that of trusted resources.

As such, this guide serves as a beginner's manual to cryptocurrency, where investors can learn to take the proper steps to smart investing. As the crypto scene advances, so do the financial backers, and they adjust to the steadily developing business sectors that stem from crypto exchanges.

The innovation behind digital money is exceptional, and as crypto gradually turns into an acceptable type of payment method against the regular currency, the opportunity to invest in the exchange is as prominent as ever.

Here, you can learn about how cryptocurrency has evolved in a short period, and with this knowledge, you may confidently make your first investment in the ever-growing digital market.

## The Concept of Cryptocurrency

By definition, digital currency is advanced or virtual cash that is obtained by cryptography. This permits crypto to be extraordinarily secure, with negligible danger of fake exchanges or the double spending of assets. Alongside its security, the monetary standards are set via blockchain technology, which is implemented by an organization of computers.

The concept of cryptography may seem a bit overwhelming but will be expanded upon in further chapters. To summarize, cryptocurrency is typically safe and secure when managed properly, which we'll discuss later on.

The main purpose of its creation was to eliminate the participation of third parties, like banks, by implementing peer-to-peer systems that manage the network.

Ordinary money, like USD or CAD, can be taken, lost, and/or falsified with genuine repercussions, which is what cryptocurrency aims to solve without a central controlling party.

Although currency today is still enjoyable, it is incredibly easy to fall into debt and lose the money you've worked tirelessly to keep and accumulate over time.

By giving the user more control over their funds, and placing the ability to trade at will in their hands, cryptocurrency allows the consumer to be responsible for themselves instead of relying on an outside service.

This same concept is behind crypto being so volatile; the marketplace never sleeps when the product is in our hands.

Price changes are imminent, whether they be for the better or worse, and despite the lows, cryptocurrency is currently experiencing all-time highs in terms of value.

This is why it is important to understand the fundamentals behind the exchange, along with the core ideals that make crypto what it is today.

**Expected Learning Outcomes**

To effectively put any form of resources into crypto, you must first grasp the basics of the system. The marketplace is continually booming with development and ideas, but none of that means anything if you don't have a clue about what's happening.

Since its foundation 10 years ago, crypto has risen overall, with gains and misfortunes being shared via web-based media stages as though they were patterns. Honestly, it is a trend—an immensely profitable trend.

Cryptocurrency will always be a consistent, yet volatile, option of currency because of the main suggestions and decisions that represent the foundation of what makes online trade successful.

Throughout this guide, several terms will be mentioned that have a direct correlation to the growth of crypto, along with suggestions about how to make wise investments.

You can expect to learn how cryptocurrency was formed, along with an expanded analysis of the blockchain network, to understand how crypto functions behind money.

This guide also talks about different types of coins and how to choose the best ones, and why cryptocurrency also works like a regular currency.

However, to understand cryptocurrency, it is important to understand what crypto is, and where it originally stemmed from.

Investment strategies will also be discussed, as well as methods you can take to lower your taxes incurred by capital gains.

This guide details methods for crypto storage, tracking your portfolio, and the math behind why all cryptocurrency is as volatile as it is.

## DISCLAIMER

Cryptocurrency is a very volatile trade, and while you may be enticed to immediately follow the trend, it is important to remember that many people lose thousands of dollars every day due to bad investments, poor advice, and a lack of judgment on their trades.

Only invest what you can afford to lose, and never invest anything more. If you wish to add on to your investment, then do so when it is affordable, or limit yourself to your profits from your initial investment.

Too many go into debt and even lose their life savings over the craze, and while it is profitable, please be cautious when trading online.

# Part One

# What is Cryptocurrency?

# Chapter 1: What Is Blockchain?

As previously mentioned, cryptocurrency is exactly what the name implies; it is a currency and a viable one at that.

People have spent the last few years trying to make crypto as publicly accessible and fundable as possible to gain popularity.

If you can find crypto at a low value, and hold that coin for some time, chances are that the fluctuation works in your favor.

The fluctuation works similarly to the stock market as well, so if you are familiar with that field, crypto trading should be an easy transition.

Even so, to understand it accurately, you need to first look at how it was founded and why it is so successful today.

This chapter will explain where cryptocurrency first came from, along with its relation to regular currency, and how it has achieved success.

Cryptocurrency is created through code, using the ever-evolving blockchain technology as the base of its foundation.

Satoshi Nakamoto—more on him later—was the first to attempt creating a crypto, founding Bitcoin, in 2009, after having released it in 2008.

Note that Satoshi Nakamoto is a pseudonym, and the real creator's name is unknown to this day.

From there, a group of excited entrepreneurs jumped in on the trend, and cryptocurrency began small, with Bitcoin shares worth mere pennies per coin.

Although his true identity is unknown, Nakamoto was the name used to sign the document known as the Bitcoin white paper, which marked the beginning of the age of digital currency.

**The Problem with Electronic Cash**

Nakamoto addresses plenty of issues with electronic cash and begins the white paper by addressing the key issues associated with electronic payments, and discussing transaction costs, as well as the constant cut-off of small transactions to favor the larger audience.

He suggests that these issues stem from relying on a third-party outlet, such as a bank, or an online service such as PayPal, which requires a great amount of trust from consumers.

The alternative he proposed would change the digital age forever; Nakamoto suggested removing the centralized third-party system.

In simpler terms, consumers would be their banks, and wouldn't have to go through another company to complete transactions.

This system was designed around the cryptographic proof, which is the form of security that laid the foundation for what is known as the blockchain.

Electronic cash also does not require authorization of payments, which makes money laundering untraceable. E-cash can also be forged and replicated at will, even with a centralized party making sure that things are running correctly.

Although electronic cash opens up new opportunities for businesses and especially small businesses, it can introduce taxation issues, unstable foreign exchange rates, a disturbed money supply, and the potential for financial crises.

The thing that makes it all worth it is the accessibility, as money can be transferred in an instant to others all over the world.

Although it is incredibly convenient, it is limited to the third party centralizing the exchange. That's what Bitcoin aimed to change for the future.

## The Timestamp

At the moment of writing, Bitcoin is worth around US$37,000. If you bought Bitcoin in 2011 when it was worth US$1 and held it for a decade, you would be living pretty well right now, and likely would be retired already.

However, it still begs the question of how exactly the transactions are recorded without a third-party system like a bank to help.

It's simple. The digital transactions are recorded by a method known as timestamps. Timestamps provide proof of a transaction's existence by recording the exact time and date that each transaction is processed.

Similar to transaction history in your bank account, it records all necessary information about the transaction, such as the amount transferred, and the number of blocks used to make that transfer possible.

Unlike banks, however, this type of information is completely public for anyone to use.

This is done to create a chronological chain of transactions, so it is easier to trace through the amount of data that is stored in a block.

In the process, the blockchain is created, and the system behind cryptocurrency slowly begins to evolve into what makes it profitable.

**What is Blockchain?**
Although it seems complicated, Blockchain technology can be broken down simply.

For starters, it is important to see blockchain as a database; a structured set of data held in a computer, especially one that is accessible in various ways.

It is a system of recording information in a way that makes it difficult to change, hack, or cheat the system, making it incredibly secure to use for monetary transactions.

Essentially, blockchain is a digital ledger of transactions that is duplicated and distributed across the entire network of computer systems on the network.

Every block contains several transactions, and every time a new transaction occurs, a record of the said transaction is added to every participant's ledger.

When multiple people manage a decentralized database, it is known as Distributed Ledger Technology, (DLT) which shows that a group of people were behind a set number of transactions.

Blockchain is a variant of DLT since transactions are recorded with a cryptographic signature known as a hash.

Cryptography is the art of writing and solving codes, and it essentially allows blockchain security to exist in the way that it does.

If someone were to change the block being used for transactions, it would be immediately apparent that the data had been tampered with.

If a hacker, for example, wanted to corrupt the blockchain system, they would have to change *every block* in the existence of the chain, as well as all of the distributed versions of the chain as well.

There are millions of blocks in circulation every day between Bitcoin and Ethereum, which is what makes it nearly impossible for a hacker to access and corrupt.

This is what allowed cryptocurrency to work against its predecessors, as digital money was nothing more than a failure in the past.

**The Many Uses of Crypto**

Cryptocurrency has a multitude of uses outside of its everyday function as a method of investment.

At the end of the day, cryptocurrency is a viable form of currency that people use to make transactions.

Crypto is just as viable as the everyday dollar, and it holds up the concepts that contribute to a valuable currency that is accepted between many buyers and consumers.

In fact, on June 9, 2021, El Salvador was the first country to make Bitcoin legal tender, i.e., an accepted method of payment by the government.

It has become so popular that some people have created online crypto casinos where many can play roulette and blackjack from the comfort of their homes.

Besides gambling, however, cryptocurrency does have many uses outside of its initial use as an investment option.

Some companies, such as Tesla (up until recently, that is), accept Bitcoin as a form of payment in exchange for their vehicles.

The form of payment was only taken down after Bitcoin suffered incredible backlash for its un-eco-friendly use of mining, as the energy consumption is too large to maintain.

Regardless, a major company had given the option to purchase vehicles in exchange for a digital coin.

That alone shows that a cryptocurrency is a viable form of payment. If the option to pay with crypto isn't there, then it can always be converted to cash using online exchanges and trades.

Most marketplace apps allow you to withdraw your funds almost instantly after getting them.

As well as investing yourself, many coins have projects behind them with great causes for the everyday world.

LO3 Energy, for example, is an eco-friendly blockchain establishment that promotes the use of solar panels instead of carbon-based power.

Users who already have solar panels can sell their credits to residents who don't have solar panel access, allowing for the use of blockchain to come into play to share solar power access with an entire community.

Eco-friendly coins have recently become more popular, thanks to Bitcoin receiving backlash for its power usage, and as such, they may prove to be good investments when the market goes back into an upswing.

Overall, there are plenty of uses for cryptocurrency besides the initial investment, and the most important thing you can do with your coins is to be as comfortable as you possibly can.

After all, no one wants to invest in something that makes them anxious.

The goal is to look for the best possible option when it is available, which is possible through crypto, but always look to invest in something that suits your values well.

**Overview**

To conclude this chapter, it is important to restate the main factor that makes cryptocurrency so popular today, which is that the market can rise just as easily as it can fall, making volatility a factor in every imaginable crypto investment.

At its peak times, cryptocurrency has a plentiful number of uses, however, the marketplace is constantly changing, which can be a major concern for any investment for all traders. Additionally, the 24/7 open market does not stop for anyone, as trades are always occurring.

Don't be fooled, however, as there is plenty to be worried about in the crypto scene, as any negative can also be found in a positive situation. 24/7 constant trading means constant price changes, where your shares can skyrocket in a matter of minutes while you are asleep at home.

The volatility and risk are what make potential investors step away from investing in cryptocurrency, even though most predict that the market will rise to all-time highs in the next five to 10 years.

That's why it is equally as important to know where to invest, and more specifically, how to invest in something worth your while. As such, it is also important to eliminate any misconceptions about the technology, as being aware of them will be to your advantage as an investor.

## Chapter 2: The Difference Between Blockchain and Cryptocurrency

Blockchain, by definition, is a decentralized, distributed ledger that records the worth of a digital asset. In other words, blockchain is what determines the value of a coin, and the technology behind it is what makes the market so volatile.

The database stores encrypted data and send it out in chains to form a source of truth for the data, keeping it in chronological order. Blockchain is also open source, allowing others to use the original code and create something out of it.

This is what causes an influx of coins to be created, as many attempts to get a piece of the profitable pie that is the digital trade.

Blockchain technology is considered revolutionary for its nearly uncrackable encryption details, making every transaction safe and secure on a level never quite seen before in the digital age.

While it may seem like a lot to take in, the technology can be simplified when breaking down how the process works.

## *Blocks*

Every chain consists of blocks, each of which has three basic elements:

- The data in the block
- The nonce—a randomly-generated 32-bit whole number that is generated when the block is created
- The hash—an extremely small 256-bit number that is connected to the nonce

Once the first block is created in the chain, the nonce is generated through cryptography and is then connected to the hash.

Afterward, the data in the block is considered to be signed and forever tied to its data until mined and retrieved by another user.

With this level of encryption, fraud and scams are put to a halt, as it is incredibly difficult for one to encrypt this level of data on their own.

### The Process of Blockchain

After the encryption is done, and the block is connected to its data, the block can be considered an asset with a monetary value attached to it.

The price value depends on the supply and demand for it, as well as the availability and competing cryptocurrencies around it.

For example, Bitcoin is so expensive because 88.5% of the total supply has been mined, giving it a high demand for users who wish to invest.

DOGE, on the other hand, is incredibly cheap because the supply is virtually limitless, with millions of coins being pumped into the marketplace every day.

As of this writing, there is currently 129 billion DOGE in circulation, compared to Bitcoin's 18 million.

That drastically changes the price, and the volatility kicks in when large traders dump their investments all once, causing the price to drop due to the new coins in supply.

After the block can be considered an asset, the asset is decentralized and is given public access through transparency and real-time changes.

However, the asset still needs trust to create a proper value, which is why a transparent ledger is needed to preserve the integrity of the asset.

A transparent ledger is essentially a method of storage that anyone can access; transparency in crypto means ease of accessibility, while a ledger is a database of shared data across some people.

The asset is being connected to a real investor's storage unit to ensure that the asset is, in fact, real and can be used for other purposes outside of the initial investment.

As Nakamoto discussed in the Bitcoin white paper, the removal of third-party help should be eliminated to create a greater transaction market through digital data.

However, removing third parties from the process would result in low security, which could open people's investments to theft.

To counter that issue, Nakamoto introduced cryptography as a method of security, which evolved into the technology known as the blockchain.

By being spread across a multitude of networks, the need for a third party was eliminated.

The security measures used, along with the public technology behind blockchain, is what make blockchain technology so prominent and enticing to new investors willing to make risky investments for better returns on their investments.

This method of trading and investing is really what put crypto in the spotlight when it was first introduced, and the research behind it is what makes it valuable in today's world of finance.

## The Difference Between Blockchain and Cryptocurrency

The terms *blockchain* and *cryptocurrency* can be difficult to understand, as the two are both correlated with and differentiated from each other.

The most important thing to understand is that the two are not the same.

Blockchain itself is not a cryptocurrency; it is simply the technology behind what makes a cryptocurrency usable and acceptable as a trading option.

To understand the technology a bit more, please examine the analogy below and follow along:

Say, for example, you go with your children to the local mall's fun zone, so they can play some games and have a little bit of fun.

You buy them some gaming tokens, which they use to play a bunch of games, and they win a lot of prizes.

After an hour of playing, both you and the children are all satisfied with your time spent, and are incredibly tired from all the running around that was done.

You decide to buy them some ice cream and call it night. However, when buying the ice cream, you notice that you still have some tickets left over from the fun zone.

Because those tickets are only acceptable in the fun zone in exchange for prizes, the tickets have no value when taken away from them, meaning that you certainly can't buy ice cream with them.

It has zero worth outside of its home, even though it has tremendous value when you go back to the fun zone to get another prize.

In this example, the gaming tickets are cryptocurrencies, and the mall's fun zone is the blockchain network.

This means that the participants that build and give the tickets a value are what's allowing them to be used in transactions.

Since Bitcoin is an application of blockchain technology, the same rules apply to the world's most popular cryptocurrency.

Since the boom in popularity, a misconception of the terms was created that made it seem as if the two were the same.

This is not the case, however, as blockchain is a groundbreaking technology that changes the digital world as we see it, and cryptocurrency just happens to be a product of that technology.

Other products of blockchain are voting polls and space technology, proving that there are more uses to it than creating digital coins in which to invest.

Cryptocurrency, at the end of the day, is an application of a larger system, known as the blockchain, which revolves around the fintech industry and all things like it.

## Overview

Understanding the technology behind what makes crypto valuable is essential to your investment if something unfortunate happens.

Although cryptography is incredibly secure, reports of hacks have happened before, mainly due to errors made by exchange sites.

To keep your investment as safe as possible, be sure to use a trusted storage option and ignore most of the ads you see on Facebook.

Typically, when a coin is being advertised, its maximum valuation has already peaked. Most likely, the exchange is looking to make some additional cash from new investors.

For example, it was only after DOGE crashed from its all-time peak of around US$0.68 that Crypto.com, an online exchange market, started promoting DOGE and SHIB, and the coin hasn't returned to its original form since.

This would cost new investors about 60% to 80% of their original investment, while the exchange would profit from the transaction fees.

The fact is, if an ad is telling you to invest in a coin, it is probably too late to put down a deposit.

## Chapter 3: The Man Behind Bitcoin

Cryptocurrency was always a popular topic but only soared to stardom when the market experienced its first bubble in 2017.

After hitting a low of US$200 in August of 2015, strong support helped the coin to reach a value of US$770 in June of 2016.

From there, the price rose to its all-time high of US$1,345 in late March of 2017, and Bitcoin would go on to enter a parabolic phase known as a bubble; another term for explosive price behavior.

By the end of the year, Bitcoin's value had skyrocketed to US$20,000, which represented 10,000 times the margin of profit in a matter of nearly two years.

That type of valuation sent the media into a frenzy over the coin, with similar events repeating themselves in 2021.

The popularity of cryptocurrency eventually spawned a multitude of investment choices besides the mainstream options, as people began to take an interest in developing and creating currencies utilizing any discretion they chose to take.

This is what sparked the evolution of crypto; a euphoria of coins was able to be traded and obtained on the spot through exchanges and online media.

People saw prices going up, and some investors were willing to take a gamble on the upcoming digital age.

Fast forward to the present day, and the same people who invested 10% of their portfolios are looking at gains of nearly 100% or higher, mainly because they chose to hold their investments and wait out the bullish market.

Although it can be enticing to jump right in, it is important to first understand the technology behind the works and to learn about exactly who the man behind the craze is.

## Satoshi Nakamoto

Satoshi Nakamoto is the name used by the creators of the Bitcoin cryptocurrency. Although the name is synonymous with Bitcoin, Nakamoto may not be a real person at all.

The actual person that the name represents has never been found, leading to people believing that the name Nakamoto is a coverup for a different identity or even a group of people.

Despite the mystery behind the name, Satoshi Nakamoto is a celebrity in the world of cryptocurrency, and to this day, it is unclear if the name refers to a group of people or just one individual.

Regardless, what is known about the man is that he published the infamous Bitcoin white paper in 2008, which jump-started the development of cryptocurrency.

Nakamoto's identity is fully clouded in mystery, and what is known about him is incredibly obscure. It is said that Nakamoto began coding Bitcoin in 2007, creating the first implementation of the crypto in C++, a common coding language used in the modern crypto world.

In August of 2008, he sent private emails to two well-respected cypherpunks, Hal Finney and Wei Dai, for feedback on the earliest versions of the Bitcoin white paper document.

A cypherpunk is someone who has studied the environment of cryptography and understands privacy-enhancing technologies, with the purpose being to promote social and political change.

Nakamoto shared his work with men who understand the field just as well as he did, and the response he got in return was overwhelmingly positive.

As previously mentioned, the Bitcoin white paper is seen as a holy manuscript in the current digital age.

Without Nakamoto's contributions, cryptocurrency would have failed to exist as it does today and would have fallen into obscurity like its predecessors.

Thanks to his research and contributions, Bitcoin was able to take off to become a platform that would change people's lives forever, all thanks to the Bitcoin white paper identifying the issues with the digital trade.

However, that paper only discusses the technology behind the scenes, and not the reason for creating it. So why then did Nakamoto choose to create Bitcoin?

## What Is Bitcoin and Why Was It Created?

The concept of Bitcoin first came into creation in 2008, as a response to the Great Financial Crisis caused by the world's reliance on banks as intermediaries of transactions.

Nakamoto had the idea of straying away from third parties, which would mean eliminating banks from the equation, opting instead to rely on a peer-to-peer payment system that did not rely on a third party to confirm the transaction.

Replacing the third party would be blockchain, the technology that records all transactions for the public to see while keeping every transaction secure and nearly impervious to scams and hacking attempts.

With this system in place, banks did not need to be involved in each and every transaction, allowing for the process of selling and buying cryptocurrency to become much more accessible in the public domain.

This method would rely on the *proof of work* system, which introduces mathematical algorithms to confirm transactions without using a central authority or a third party to act as a middle man.

Instead, the technology behind the works acted as the middle man, which is why blockchain is a major contributor to how cryptocurrency operates today.

**Overview**

After Bitcoin was created in 2009 by Nakamoto, a small number of people got behind the idea and eventually formed a company around it.

It took time, and in 2011, Bitcoin hit a US$1 valuation, an incredible improvement from the two years' prior valuation of US$0.

The eventual evolution of cryptocurrency is what sparked others to join in an attempt to make a profit through blockchain, and so new coins were pushed onto the market like never before.

It would also inspire others to explore blockchain technology themselves, creating new methods of blockchain and evolving the technology along the way.

A great example of this is Ethereum, an open-source coin based on smart contract functionality.

In August of 2015, while Bitcoin was worth around US$330, Ethereum stepped onto the market trading at around US$2.77.

Ethereum would go on to be the second biggest cryptocurrency, currently valued at US$2,188, and thus obtaining the status of the world's most actively used blockchain.

The introduction of cryptocurrency would not have been possible without Nakamoto, despite the unknown facts about him.

His gender is even a mystery, and he is only considered to be a male because of his P2P Foundation profile.

Nonetheless, the introduction of the peer-to-peer system (or P2P, for short) sparked massive support for the digital trade, enticing others to jump into the trendy cryptocurrency wave.

However, many make such trades blindly, and dump their money wherever possible, hoping for a short-term return on their investment.

It is important to understand the type of coins that are on the market, as well as what coins are viable to invest in, and why there are so many cryptocurrencies in the first place.

# Chapter 4: The Different Types of Cryptocurrency

Cryptocurrency, at its core, is a list of options that any individual can invest in at a moment's notice.

Most of these coins are generated through mining, which is a process that involves using blockchain to create crypto without an initial down payment or investment in a digital exchange.

This helps the crypto scene stand out against other major trading options since bull runs make it look like money is growing on trees (or in this case, computers, and hard drives).

In reality, that is far from the case, and it is ultimately hurtful and dangerous to the environment to manage constantly running crypto mines.

The energy used to maintain the works is substantial, at best, but this method of creation is what spawned a multitude of cryptocurrency options, and is a major benefactor of placing cryptocurrency in the position it is in today.

With a multitude of coins to select from, choosing one to invest in can be overwhelming, yet the process can be very simple if appropriate effort and research are applied.

Before making that investment, however, a few things need to be established.

Firstly, it is important to remember that cryptocurrency is an incredibly volatile and risky form of investment, as the market changes drastically every day.

Your investment can double overnight, and you can also lose 50% of it in the same time frame.

As a prime example, my portfolio has gained or lost thousands of dollars overnight! It would be great to be able to sell every time you hit a high and buy every time you hit a low, but I am typically lazy when it comes to doing that.

There will be more about your investment and how to manage it later on in this guide, but always remember to invest within your risk-loss ratio; make a line between what you're willing to invest and what you're willing to lose.

## Types of Cryptocurrency

There are currently over 4,500 cryptocurrencies to choose from, however, many of these have little to no value. Four years ago, there were only 1,000 coins in circulation.

The reason for the influx of coins is due to how blockchain technology works. By being open-source, any developer can use the original code to create something unique out of it, and developers continue the practice to this day.

Surging prices have led many to try to get a cut of the action, allowing for more investment options to be available all over the world.

On top of that, nearly all cryptocurrency trades take place online, meaning that everything is incredibly easy to access and use.

This is what inspired many to try their hand at creating cryptocurrencies.

Thanks to the open-source blockchain technology, many were enticed to jump on the bandwagon to attempt to profit from the digital age.

Part of the reason for the surge resides behind the technology, however, another reason relies on the relative ease of open-source work.

Open-source code is code that anyone can take and use for their purposes, allowing others to create another build around the conceptual Bitcoin model.

Ethereum is an example of such, as the network was developed to be used as a way to create your own personal digital coins.

Other times, forks are created in the software code that changes the way that crypto is governed, and incidentally, creates new crypto altogether.

Bitcoin Cash, for example, was created in 2017 as a result of a Bitcoin fork allowing for more transactions to be recorded on a single blockchain (Note: More of these terms will be expanded upon in further chapters; use this chapter as a slow introduction to the concepts behind those that make up the marketplace).

While some coins may be nothing more than a bubble waiting to pop, the decentralized nature of the technology, and the broad scope of how it can be applied in the software world, is in itself a reason why there are so many cryptocurrencies.

The community also plays a factor in what makes cryptocurrency so popular today, with social media accounts dedicated to the trade and their favorite coins.

It is as if cryptocurrency is a profitable commodity that entices users to trade their investments to others for different coins at the ease of a button push.

When the market goes on a downswing, everybody suffers, and when the market rises back up, everybody celebrates.

It also promotes the creation of other cryptocurrencies that play off of popular trends.

Dogecoin, for example, was created as a joke that caught on fire in 2021, allowing for it to skyrocket in the price for a few months before settling back at an investor's medium.

People only lose money in cryptocurrency investments when they sell too early due to losses or invest at a price that is too high for the current market.

The strategy of crypto is similar to many other investments, that being to buy low and sell high, and people tend to forget that when investing in such a volatile market.

## Ethereum 101

As previously mentioned, Ethereum is a blockchain software platform that allows users to create their own blockchain algorithm.

From this, the spawn of multiple cryptocurrencies occurred, as everyone tried to jump in to make the next Bitcoin.

Ethereum, however, is a coin of itself, launching in 2015 with a valuation of US$2.77 and eventually dropping as low as US$0.68.

It rose to popularity after going against the concept of Bitcoin's security by allowing both permission and permissionless transactions.

The expansion of the P2P system allowed for the average block time to be cut down to 12 seconds, in comparison to Bitcoin's lengthy 10 minutes.

Other than those interface changes, Ethereum is also built on the blockchain idea, with users being allowed to send and receive Ethereum without a third party stepping in the way.

Allowing the Ethereum platform to expand the P2P system was the company's answer to Nakamoto's currency issue discussed in the Bitcoin white paper, which is what enticed investors to buy in and bet on the next wave of crypto technology.

At the moment of writing, Ethereum is worth US$2,338 and is the second most popular cryptocurrency on the market, which makes it crucial to understand what makes the platform so great for cryptocurrency and blockchain technology.

**Ethereum Smart Contracts**

Ethereum is built around smart contracts, and to understand Ethereum smart contracts, you first must grasp the concept of what a smart contract is.

Smart contracts are computer programs and protocols that can ensure a digital contract between the two parties, those being buyer and seller, and what should be expected on those terms.

In this way, smart contracts can create financial transactions, send messages to other users, and lay out the rules and litigations of said transactions.

These run on several blockchain networks, with Ethereum taking advantage and becoming one of the largest networks to run the operation.

It also can help reduce the cost of traditional contracts that run outside of a blockchain network, while also promoting the usage of cryptocurrency and DLT.

With 1.5 million smart contracts available on the Ethereum platform alone, the company continues to advance the technology behind blockchain, while enhancing cryptography as the trade evolves.

However, there are downsides to the cause. For example, expanding the P2P system makes the chronological order of transactions difficult to manage, since blocks of data are being stored at 10 times the speed of Bitcoin blocks.

Also, Ethereum's activity is far less than Bitcoins and has a long way to go before it gets to compete at a high scale against it.

Yes, Ethereum is the second most popular cryptocurrency in the world and is a great coin with all due respect, but it needs an additional value of US$38,000 before it even comes close to being a major competitor to its opponent.

That being said, Ethereum smart contracts are widely considered an excellent addition to the world of cryptocurrency and blockchain coding.

As the name suggests, it is a process that involves smart contracts that run on top of the company's main network, allowing for transactions to take place at a faster pace.

This is possible thanks to the open-source code that blockchain allows, and so Ethereum was born as a product of Bitcoin's original code.

One of the main use cases related to the company is related to the fact that it efficiently supports smart contracts.

During the last few years, several firms and companies were leveraging the features implemented by Ethereum to write their contracts, protocols, and networks.

A coin-based solution around eliminating the third party was helping the third parties to become more secure themselves, which was a great move for the company to take.

Now, with global support from all institutions, Ethereum has become accepted as a viable cryptocurrency that many believe will take over Bitcoin when the mining phase takes its toll.

The Ethereum network works with the ETH cryptocurrency, currently the second largest in the world to Bitcoin, which is an important element to understanding why the peer expansion was so effective.

There are thousands of blockchain networks and digital assets on the market, and Ethereum was able to get in early in 2015, expand its user system for nearly all forms of transactions, and gain the trust of millions of users.

This surged their valuation through the roof, with the coin never falling under US$1,000 since the beginning of 2021.

**What Is Monero? (XMR)**
Monero, also known as the coin XMR, was among the first cryptocurrency to implement the security of cryptography.

To simplify, it was one of the first cryptos to follow the footsteps of the Bitcoin outline.

It differentiated itself by allowing users to send and receive transactions without the block data being public.

The Bitcoin outline allowed transaction data to be public and accessible, being the amount exchanged between transactions as well as data about the sender and receiver.

Monero instead chose to make that data private, creating the first of many privacy coins of the era.

Privacy coins are just as the name implies; they are coins that promote privacy and control over the user's data. By doing this, users were enticed to have even more control over their transactions and avoided having their data be public.

As such, Monero is often classed with other privacy coins such as Zcash (ZEC) that have sought to address the privacy weaknesses of Bitcoin.

This begs the question of how privacy coins work, and how do they differentiate themselves from other coins that stay consistent with the original Bitcoin outline, keeping their data public along the process?

**Privacy Coins and How They Work**
Privacy coins were a revolutionary addition to the development of cryptocurrency. The way that they work and how they differentiate themselves from normal cryptocurrencies is explained here.

Varying these coins works in several different ways, but the end goal is always the same.

Privacy coins are designed to hide details that normal cryptocurrencies make available, such as digital addresses and amounts transacted so it is incredibly difficult to piece together which parties participated in a transaction.

This level of security is so tight, in fact, that it is nearly impossible for it to be breached. So, how exactly is that privacy implemented?

Privacy coins, such as Monero, create a new, single-use address for each transaction known as a *stealth address* so that there is no apparent way to link multiple transactions to a single source.

After the address is used, it is ditched and is continuously replaced by another stealth address to cover up the true digital address of the transaction.

In this way, only the sender and receiver can determine where the payment is sent, enhancing security and the trust of the P2P system along the way.

Monero also uses ring signatures, a method adopted by other coins.

In this case, ring signatures string together multiple user addresses without revealing which address is ultimately signed.

This was another revolution created to crack down on privacy, including the addition of stealth addresses.

Other streamline blockchains, such as Mimblewimble, are designed to keep a more compact history than traditional blockchains and don't reveal any identifying information to the public.

For Bitcoin buyers who wish to ensure a more private trade, a process known as CoinJoin is used, which mixes together transactions of various senders and then disburses the funds across recipients to blur transactions together.

Another technique used is called Zero-Knowledge Succinct Non-Interactive Argument of Knowledge and is also known as zk-SNARK.

It sounds like a lot, so we will stick with the abbreviated term. zk-SNARK technology uses advanced cryptography to encrypt identifying information.

This technique was implemented by the coin Zcash to solve the anonymity problem with the original Bitcoin blockchain where people could be identified by comparing their data to other transactions on the blockchain.

Zcash aimed to crack down on that privacy, and as such, zk-SNARK was born.

The protocol uses something called *zero-knowledge proof*, which allows both parties of a transaction to verify each other without revealing private information.

Most types of proof, on the other hand, require at least one other party to have all of the information available. Zcash's implementation of the zk-SNARK system allowed for the coin to become prominent today and is a great option for people looking to keep their information as private as possible.

## Ripple Definition

Ripple, also known as XRP, is a technology that acts as both a cryptocurrency and a digital payment for financial transactions.

First released in 2012 by Chris Larsen and Jed McCaleb, Ripple's main process was built around the SWIFT system, which works with international transfers.

The goal was to create a payment, or asset, settlement exchange as well as a remittance system. It does this by operating through open-source platforms as well as by implementing a peer-to-peer trading system.

This allows for a shameless transfer of money in any form, expanding the trade outside of a country's local currency.

That also includes cryptocurrencies, meaning you can trade your Bitcoin shares for a piece of XRP (at the time of writing, 1 Bitcoin is worth the equivalent of XRP$25,854, so people tend to sell a fraction of Bitcoin for a better investment price).

This expansive system introduced the concept of converting cryptocurrencies for others, which exchanges such as Binance have implemented today as a quality-of-life improvement.

What differentiates Ripple, however, is its connection to third-party interference.

Since Ripple's focus is on monetary exchange and is reliant on being a global payment network, the company counts major banks and financial services among its reliable customers.

It does this by implementing the coin, XRP, in its products, which ensures a quick conversion between currencies for third-party customers.

Although the original Bitcoin outline looked to eliminate third parties from the equation, Ripple allows them to be a part of the process by working as an exchange platform for all currencies, whether crypto-related or not.

This is great for the cryptocurrency economy, as it makes converting and investing a much simpler process than they used to be.

**IOTA and the Machine Economy**
IOTA is a DLT that allows for multiple participants in the network to transact value and data through a shared ledger.

Their data structure, known as Tangle, is a permissionless public network, meaning that anyone can join without permission.

They pride themselves on an advanced data protocol that focuses on open, fee-less data. IOTA has marketed itself as the backbone of IOTA, though it may be more apt to describe it as the backbone of the machine economy.

It acts as a trust layer and automation enabler and provides infrastructure for the entire semantic web so that the machine economy can run efficiently.

Their goal is to advertise a unified identity, which they dub *The Solution*, by creating a machine economy that is dependent on the economy of things, real-time transactions, and digital trust.

To do so, they create a unified identity that is based on public, permissionless, fee-less, and open source.

In theory, their outline eliminates a lot of problems that the original Bitcoin template failed to fix, such as long block times, by introducing one-time signatures and secure data transfers.

They also implement these variables while maintaining a low resource requirement, which allows other components of the technology to work more efficiently.

This allows for a safer, and more secure, method of storing and obtaining data.

As a coin, IOTA is currently priced at US$0.86 and is a great investment for those seeking to find something for the future, as IOTA consistently places itself to be the next to advance the world of cryptocurrency.

**Overview**

Different types of cryptocurrencies make investing easier, so long as your research is done, and yet, there are still coins that fall outside of the typical standards of what a coin is supposed to represent.

Some coins are simply variants of other cryptocurrencies, and others were made just for fun without a chance of proper valuation.

Even so, it is important to address all aspects of the cryptocurrency market, as many people have made great sums of money by investing in these coins before they became trendy.

## Chapter 5: Meme Coins—What Are They?

Has your grandson ever shown you a picture of a cute dog, and you thought to yourself, *Man, that dog is cute, but it is not like there's any value in this picture outside of the humor it brings?* Well, in the world of cryptocurrency, that fact is half-true.

The general public has recently taken a liking to Meme coins, and they exploded in popularity during March of 2021, which incidentally, raised the prices of those coins to all-time highs.

People who bought coins as commodities to share with friends were now seeing actual returns on their investments, thanks to a social media craze that sent the world into a frenzy.

What exactly are memes, and how exactly have meme coins changed a crucial part of cryptocurrency history?

## What Are Meme Coins?

Memes are a form of simple humor that is posted all over the internet.

They are incredibly popular and act as a way for social media members to communicate without having to text, such as sending funny pictures to one another.

Meme coins were created as a subcategory to memes; they have no inherent value, other than being a commodity, as they are themed around internet jokes.

In theory, they shouldn't be profitable at all, yet people saw large increases in their portfolios by simply pushing the jokes farther than they typically could go.

A good example of this is the original meme coin, known as Dogecoin (also known as DOGE).

Based on the popular Dogecoin meme, which originated with a picture of a Shiba Inu dog, the creators of Dogecoin looked to introduce some light humor to the ever-evolving world of cryptocurrency.

Running on its blockchain network, Dogecoin was distinguishable from other cryptocurrencies that relied on an existing blockchain.

That's right, developers Billy Markus and Jackson Palmer created their blockchain code and cryptocurrency in 2013, all for the sake of poking fun at the craze that was, and still is, cryptocurrency.

Placing itself as a joke, however, was all a part of their marketing strategy.

Markus and Palmer wanted to create a coin that could reach a broader demographic than Bitcoin while staying away from the controversy that most cryptocurrencies faced at the time.

As such, they chose to create a coin based around a meme everyone knew and dubbed it the *fun and friendly internet currency*.

The enticing thing about Dogecoin, and other meme coins like it, was how inexpensively a share could be purchased.

In December of 2013, Dogecoin was worth a mere US$0.00026. At the time of writing, Dogecoin is valued at US$0.30.

Consider the valuation for a moment; if you bought US$500 worth of Dogecoin in 2016 when it was worth US$0.000227, you would see a maximum increase of 237,000% when Dogecoin hit its all-time peak on May 8, 2021, of US$0.54.

That would turn your US$500 investment into approximately US$1,000,000 worth of Dogecoin. People jokingly see meme coins as the next cryptocurrency to catch on fire, and the low prices are what makes it enticing.

This begs the question that remains prominent today of what else makes meme coins popular, and if anything, are they a good investment option?

**Why Are They Popular?**
Meme coins gain popularity through viral social media trends, which is another contributing factor to what makes meme coins so enticing.

Their value is placed directly in the consumer's hand, eliminating the concept of supply and demand. We previously briefed how there is essentially an unlimited amount of Dogecoin available on the market, giving the supply an incredibly low value.

This is what created the coin's original value at US$0.00023—with so much to go around, of course, the price would be low.

However, thanks to internet trends, fan pages for the coin, and the introduction of Tik Tok sensations, consumers have created an all-time high demand for Dogecoin.

As such, because it is popular and trendy, the demand overweighs the concept of supply, surging the price upwards and allowing people to make an incredible profit on Dogecoin investments.

The downside of meme coin investments is that they must be considered as incredibly short term, as all trends must eventually die and leave demand at another low.

You may have to wait a long time to get a decent return, however, there are times when you don't have to wait at all.

Due to the surge in popularity, others saw an opportunity to jump on the layout created by Dogecoin's developers, which led to the introduction of the crypto subcategory, Meme coins.

As of today, there are 80 Meme coins and tokens listed on the popular price aggregator, CoinMarketCap.

Many imitate Dogecoin's original concept to the core, creating coins based around cute animals that are derived from internet culture.

An example of this is imitator Shibu Inu, also known as SHIB coin, which was built using Ethereum's open-source platform and based itself around the Shiba Inu breed of dog instead of the meme Dogecoin looked to capitalize on.

Imitator coins like to capitalize when the trend for a Meme coin is very popular, to earn money through people looking for the next big thing.

When the trend dies, however, so do the prices of imitator coins, as the markets are always directly correlated to one another.

SHIB coins' all-time high was around US$0.0000364 when the Dogecoin trend was soaring.

When the trend was over, however, it lost nearly 80% of that value within the time frame of a few months, leaving SHIB coin at a current recovering price of US$0.0000084—a massive loss for investors.

I currently own about 49 Million SHIB coins. My cost was about $400 in total. One of these days, if the price even reaches $.01, I will be sitting on $490,000 for a $400 investment.

I look at crypto as an investment, just like stocks. As long as my crypto is bought cheaply enough, I don't care how long I have to hold it.

People tend to worry when they see that they missed the "high point" to sell and that they lost money. Did they really? As long as you can sell for more than you bought, you did not lose money!

A case in point. Years ago, a Japanese company called Softbank, began to market its shares. I had been watching them for a while and when they first offered shares at $69, I bought 1000 shares.

They were a DOT com powerhouse and within a year, their shares were trading at $2100 a share. And then came the crash. Overnight, their shares plummeted to $800 a share.

I sold my shares and put $800,00 in the bank, but my friends were all moaning that I had lost over a million dollars ($1.3 million to be exact).

When I told them that I did not lose money, but made $731,000, they couldn't understand it. Buying and holding crypto can be the same thing.

My son in Florida got me into crypto when he asked me to loan him $10,000 to buy a miner to mine bitcoin, in 2012. I had to do a lot of investigating to get the information I needed to start mining, myself.

In April 2017, Charlie decided to cash in a good chunk of his coins to buy his house. Bitcoin was selling at $1013  Later that year, Bitcoin hit its all-time high of $13,062.

My son then complained to me that if he hadn't sold his coins to buy his house, he would be sitting on $5.4 Million.

I explained to him that if I had just bought Bitcoin with the 10,000 dollars (2000 BTC) that I gave him to start mining, I would be sitting on $26,548,000 million. At its all-time high in 2021, 2000 BTC would be worth $122,000,000 Million. It's all relative.

Other meme coins are created as plain gimmicks looking to capitalize on whatever is popular in the mainstream internet media.

In May of 2021, for example, Facebook CEO Mark Zuckerberg posted a picture of his pet goats captioned *My Goats: Max and Bitcoin.* Soon after, a meme token dubbed *Aqua Goat* saw an increase of 300% within hours of Zuckerberg's original post.

The coin is not directly related to Zuckerberg's post, but the consumer market demanded a coin that was related to the trend, and they used Aqua Goat as its coin to represent them.

Elon Musk, the founder of Tesla, is another name that is prominent in the world of meme coins, considering that he is also a celebrity among crypto investors.

Not only did he influence the surging trend that was Dogecoin, but he also has coins dedicated to him due to various comments he has made on social media.

On the Twitter platform, Musk tweeted that if there were ever a scandal about him, it should be known as *Elongate* by popular media.

Within hours, an ELONGATE token was launched, with profit only happening if and when Elon Musk finds himself in controversy.

The motives may have been mercenary; however, the developers of the ELONGATE token claim to have donated $3 million of their profits to charities of their choosing.

**Overview**
The community is truly what makes cryptocurrency so popular today, with social media accounts dedicated to the trade and their favorite coins.

For meme coins specifically, cryptocurrency is a profitable commodity that entices users to trade their investments to others for different coins at the ease of a button push.

When the market goes on a downswing, everybody suffers, and when the market rises back up, everybody celebrates. The same can be applied to whatever is trendy at the time.

People lose money in cryptocurrency investments when the trend collapses or they panic-sell their losses, and despite the downsides, meme coins are incidentally placed as a way to bring crypto traders together.

## Chapter 6: A Fork Isn't Something You Eat With!

The strategy of crypto is similar to many other investments, that being to buy low and sell high, and people tend to forget that when investing in such a volatile market.

Thanks to blockchain technology, many were enticed to jump on the bandwagon to attempt to profit from the digital age. From mainstream options to commodities, cryptocurrency has evolved into an excellent marketplace.

However, some wished to create coins directly related to the mainstream options, so that users would be able to invest in the technology of the coin without having to sacrifice the current price to own a share.

As such, cheaper alternatives to Bitcoin, such as Litecoin, were created to entice users even more, with the valuations having the limitless potential to rise over the years from conception onward.

This was made possible because Bitcoin and Ethereum run on open-source software, and when a community makes a change to that protocol, a different cryptocurrency can be created in the process.

This type of cryptocurrency is known as a fork; a coin based upon the blockchain data of another coin and is important in the cryptocurrency market today.

## What Is a Fork?

A fork is created whenever a community makes a change to the blockchain's protocol or basic set of rules.

When this happens, the chain splits, creating a second blockchain that shares all of its histories with the original, but is headed off in a new direction.

This allows for the forked coin to be directly related to the protocols of the original source code.

This doesn't mean that their predecessors aren't viable investments; however, it does allow for a coin to evolve within itself, allowing for fork coins to be proof of the change to the crypto economy.

Sometimes fork coins are a result of changes or improvements to a currency's network, which means that forks are ultimately security enhancers or proof of a plausible update.

Other times, however, a developer may be looking to use a fork to create entirely new crypto ecosystems.

This differentiates the type of fork coins that exist, resulting in them being split between two categories.

## Soft Forks

Say for example, that during development, new rules are introduced to crack down on security breaches.

If 75% of people choose to follow these rules, then a majority of the coins' blockchain network is being updated to new protocols and is following along as it should.

If for whatever reason, the message doesn't reach everybody, then 25% of people are not following those rules and continue to implement the old software code into the new one.

Essentially, a divide has occurred between the community behind the coin; one wants to change and another wants to stay the same.

Due to those complications, a *fork* is created that differentiates the two coins

One implementing the new changes and one acting out the original coins' white paper. In this case, the leftover portions of data are what create a soft fork, as well as evaluate its value and worth from the original blockchain source code.

Soft forks are the result of an upgrade to a blockchain's original features, and as long as it is adopted by all users, it can become a currency's new set of standards.

They can also be created as a result of developers not noticing an update, resulting in them breaking a protocol that they weren't aware of.

Essentially, if a blockchain is following the old rules, but violating the new ones, a soft fork in the coin is created.

## Hard Forks

A hard fork, however, is different from a soft fork in a multitude of ways. These forks occur when the original code has changed so much that the new version is no longer backward-compatible with earlier blocks.

Thus, to preserve resources, the blockchain splits into two, and a hard fork is created.

Hard forks are an entirely new cryptocurrency, with their own blockchain source behind them powering their valuation and affordability.

In this instance, the two blockchain source codes live together in harmony, as both are created to follow new rules and procedures.

This is why a soft fork works in one blockchain network, whereas hard forks result in a splitting of the original code, resulting in two blockchain networks.

Another difference between the two is security, as developers would rather implement a hard fork instead of a soft fork to ensure security enhancements.

This is because recording the blocks in a blockchain requires a tremendous amount of power, but the privacy gained from a hard fork makes more sense than using a soft fork.

Hard forks also allow for an entire second cryptocurrency to be implemented as a result of the original blockchain split, which makes both coins valuable to each other, rather than becoming direct competition.

## Bitcoin Cash

Bitcoin Cash, also known as BCH, is an example of a fork creating a secondary cryptocurrency deprived of its original form.

According to the development website, the original Bitcoin model was aged and unreliable, creating an opportunity for a fork, since the community could not agree on a model after the cryptocurrency crash of 2017.

Afterward, Bitcoin's dominance fell from 95% to 40%, which was mainly because of the accessibility problems of online trade. Thus, Bitcoin Cash was created, and the fork occurred on August 1, 2017.

This allowed Bitcoin to have an alternative version that made use of its new features, rules, and development roadmap.

Anyone who was a Bitcoin holder at the time also became an owner of Bitcoin Cash, so even though the two sides were at odds with each other, everybody ended up winning in the long run.

Since Bitcoin Cash was created after Bitcoin's potential skyrocketed, the two coins were priced at hefty amounts.

When introduced, Bitcoin Cash was priced around US$452, and as previously mentioned, all Bitcoin owners received Bitcoin Cash as a result of the fork.

This proved to pay out incredibly well, as, in December of 2017, Bitcoin Cash hit an all-time high of US$4,355.

Selling then was probably the best move for most investors, since the spike didn't last very long, and Bitcoin Cash resides today at a comfortable US$513.

### *Ethereum Classic*

As discussed earlier, smart contracts are what make Ethereum a viable option against its competitor, Bitcoin.

Decentralized Autonomous Organization (DAO), however, is just as prominent as smart contracts, since the governance of a DAO is codified and doesn't require any human intervention.

This sounds great, theoretically, yet a problem occurred during a 2016 DAO project titled *The DAO*. The project was a success and raised over US$150 million in crowdfunding.

However, thanks to a loophole in the smart contracts, hackers were able to get away with stealing a third of that crowdfunding profit.

US$50 million was lost in the process, which led to panic on the Ethereum platform.

After all, after having US$50 million stolen from underneath them, Ethereum realized that they needed to crack down on security harder than before.

Founders, Vitalik Buterin and Gavin Wood, proposed a radical change to the blockchain's base protocol, which would result in a hard fork of the current cryptographic code.

Although the community had immense support for this decision, some stuck to the *Code of Law* principle that Ethereum users prided themselves on.

Thus, a hard fork in the Ethereum code was created, with the updated protocols being applied to today's ETH chain, allowing the old protocols to existing as a new coin called Ethereum Classic (also known as ETC).

**Overview**

Cryptocurrency continues to evolve within itself, as evidenced by the addition of forks into blockchain technology.

By introducing forks, investors were given the option to invest in a version of a popular coin without having to spend a ridiculous amount to own a share in the original coin.

Bitcoin has Bitcoin Cash and Litecoin, for example, as hard forks of Bitcoin's original source code.

Other coins, such as Ethereum, have hard forks, like Ethereum Classic, and coins based around promoting their platform, like crypto coin Polygon, which is based on the Ethereum social platform,

One thing to remember is that forks are directly related to their original counterparts.

This means that the price changes of each coin are similar to one another, considering that the blockchain code behind them derives from one another.

When the price of Bitcoin changes, Litecoin and Bitcoin Cash prices are meant to follow, and vice versa.

The same situation applies to Ethereum forks as well; the only difference being that Polygon works as a separate entity from the Ethereum platform, instead opting to be a digitized currency of the Ethereum social network. This means that the prices are still connected, but the changes aren't as drastic as other coin forks.

Moving on, we will discuss the use of services that are available through a certain technology known as *decentralized finance*, which is a method that Ethereum uses to promote itself to push the cryptocurrency market to all sorts of heights.

## Chapter 7: Decentralized Finance and the DeFi Revolution

The crypto economy is booming, and as a result, the market is expanding to introduce new options and methods of holding and selling cryptocurrency.

Right now, exchanges are taking steps to allow users the ability to lend, borrow, long and short, earn interest, and more on their platforms, which is beneficial for all users and shareholders alike.

A lot of these changes have been made possible thanks to a technology known as Decentralized Finance, or DeFi for short.

This is what allows for the always open, volatile markets to exist and also enables exchanges to remain dominant throughout the digital age.

It permits others to find their own ways to profit, like how some crypto-savvy Argentinians have used the technology to escape crippling inflation or how people can take out millions of dollars in loans without having to share personal identification. Regardless, the technology is remarkable and should be understood and recognized as such.

Decentralized finance, or DeFi for short, is a collective term for financial services that are available to anyone who can use the Ethereum network, which is anyone who has an internet connection.

With DeFi, the markets are always open and there are no centralized authorities to block payments or deny access to the network.

This allows for services that were originally slow and at risk of error to be automatically controlled by safer and more secure code that anyone can inspect.

The service essentially acts as an open financial system that was meant for the digital era, giving users an alternative to stock options and trading puts.

As the services are available at all hours, users have complete control and visibility of their market and everyone else's.

As well, users are given exposure to different currencies and banking options. Tens of billions of trades flow through these applications daily, with nearly no issues or problems with security or hack and data breaches.

## DeFi Versus Traditional Finance

DeFi aims to solve many problems that traditional finance fails to address, such as:

- Inability to access, or lack of access, to financial services

Some people do not have the privilege of accessing banks or other financial services that can benefit their money management plans.

Thanks to DeFi, however, so long as you have an internet connection, you can control your money, income, and accounts from a mobile phone or a home computer.

- Protocols that block payment

Typical security protocols kick in that may slow down payment, or block payment to your account entirely.

With DeFi, this problem is eliminated through the use of digital addresses and the peer-to-peer system, where confirmation from both parties must be verified before funds are sent digitally to each other.

- Hidden charges to a financial account

Many bank accounts connected with savings plans and other benefits typically have rules that incur hidden charges.

This can be caused by anything from exceeding a spending limit to transferring funds from one account to another.

DeFi exchanges have no said hidden charges, with all amounts in your account being yours down to the penny.

There are no extra charges, no customer support wait lines, and no delayed payments or missing funds either.

- Government and centralized control

Traditional finance involves trusting third-party companies to manage, or in some cases mismanage your money.

Mistakes are made due to human error and can be a frustrating dilemma to deal with.

This problem is eliminated by DeFi because the individual controls their own funds. Every single penny in your account belongs to you and you only, until you choose to buy or sell your trades and options.

Giving the user full control eliminates the process of banks and other systems like it, making for a faster interface powered by user control.

- Limited trading hours

Traditional finance entities, like stock markets, have limits on availability because employees only work at certain times of the day.

This results in markets being open from 9:30 a.m. to 4:00 p.m. closed on weekends and only having access to longer times through after-hours trading.

With DeFi, there is no closing time, as the market is always open as there is no human interference behind the market's operating systems.

Instead, everything is controlled through code and digital AI, keeping the markets available on a 24/7 basis.

This is also why the markets are volatile, as everything is constantly changing with no rest.

- Long wait times for money transfers

Human processes turn money transfers into tedious tasks. Take the e-transfer system, for example, which requires case-sensitive passwords to be shared between users for money to be verified and exchanged.

This process can make the whole ordeal frustrating, especially if you deposit on a weekend, where many banks will hold your funds until the next available business day.

With DeFi and the 24/7 market, as well as the incredibly fast peer-to-peer system, money transfers are nearly instantaneous after verification, which is also a very fast process.

- Paying a premium fee to utilize better options

Online exchanges through traditional finance may require a premium fee to get better options.

For example, a monthly bank payment for a premium savings account is an increased payment that banks require for financial advantages.

DeFi accounts are all open and available with no premium payments required. All premium payments of any form are optional to the user.

The main advantage of DeFi, along with the benefits in comparison to traditional finance, is that it is built around what cryptocurrencies such as Bitcoin originally set out to eliminate.

That is, the system is built on transparency by eliminating third parties.

Financial institutions are closed books; you can't ask to see the loan history or a record of managed assets.

With DeFi, anyone in the world can look at the data and understand how the system works.

Cryptocurrency and DeFi, at their cores, are self-educated processes, with many traders learning more and more about the evolving market scene with every day that they check their accounts.

**Why Use DeFi?**

The first DeFi application was Bitcoin (you can now understand why the model is so popular), which stood out with its independent control on the network, eliminating the necessity for third-party trust.

It also introduced DeFi lending, a process that allowed users to make money or crypto the same way that banks do, with the main difference and attraction being the decentralized environment where it takes place.

When a user deposits crypto into a De-Fi platform, 100% of the interest earned on the deposit goes directly to the user, instead of a central entity in place that takes a portion of the earnings as a service fee.

Since cryptocurrency investments don't involve the use of a third party, taking out a cryptocurrency loan does not show up on your credit history unless you use a credit card to complete the transaction.

This makes borrowing through a DeFi lending platform very beneficial in cases where you need money urgently, but don't wish to sell any assets.

There are Dex DeFis, also known as DEXes, are transactions that take place without an intermediary. This means that users can trade crypto peer-to-peer without the introduction of a centralized party or middleman to oversee the transaction.

When using DEX to trade, there is no need to enter any personal details, since nearly all cryptocurrency transactions are covered by pseudonyms.

It also means that there is no central point of failure that could be breached by hackers, so long as users remain in control of their assets and trades throughout the entire transaction process.

## DeFi Growth

DeFi has its merits, but the digital age is full of quick start-ups that have not panned out as well. How can we be sure that DeFi really is the revolution that it claims to be?

Let's consider that by looking into the numbers that make up the user-positive system that DeFi runs on—Ethereum.

By the end of 2020, the DeFi movement saw significant growth in the Ethereum ecosystem, with over 130 million ETH addresses being registered into the network.

That does not include the increasing 100,000 daily new addresses in the last quarter of the year. Evidently enough, DeFi growth is real, and the numbers back it up.

According to a consensus report, over 1,195,000 unique Ethereum addresses have interacted with DeFi platforms, with over 600,000 new addresses being added in the final quarter of 2020.

This is a clear indication of the growth that confirms that DeFi continues to gain popularity to create a bigger name for itself in the crypto world.

These statistics underline the power and significance of the DeFi movement, as well as showcase what the future holds.

In time, the movement will enter the mainstream and thrive as it expands through evolving technology.

With multiple-use cases and major DeFi platforms already established, we are clearly witnessing the beginning of a new revolution in the world of online finance.

### Overview

Decentralized finance is everything that makes the cryptocurrency scene so enticing, providing users with an experience unlike any other.

By introducing a 24/7 open market, as well as creating Ethereum services that are accessible to anyone on the platform, DeFi looks to go nowhere else but up for years to come.

As we close Part 1 of this guide, let's look over some main points and topics that we have covered:

- Cryptocurrency is run on a network known as a blockchain, which makes data transfers more private and secure by encouraging peer-to-peer transactions without the use of third parties.
- Blockchain and cryptocurrency are two separate terms that correlate to one another. They are not the same thing.
- Bitcoin was implemented through the *proof of work* system discussed in the famous document known as Bitcoin white paper.
- There are different types of cryptocurrencies, ranging from mainstream options to meme coins, to forks.
- Nearly all exchanges run on DeFi technology, which makes all of the aforementioned options possible.

Part 2 of this guide will discuss investing in cryptocurrency, as well as holding your options, where to buy crypto, and knowing which coins to buy.

Remember that nearly all of the information provided in Part 1 will apply to Part 2, so don't feel discouraged if you must go back and forth between chapters to ensure comprehension.

Cryptocurrency investing is similar to traditional stocks in numerous ways, but the online environment can be difficult to navigate.

Continue reading this guide, and you'll find that the digital investment era isn't as difficult to navigate or as convoluted as some other investors may make it out to be, so long as you follow the right steps.

# Part Two Investing in Cryptocurrency

# Chapter 8: The Law of Averages

The law of averages refers to a concept that states that probability influences everyday life so that, over the long term, the possible outcomes of a repeated event occur within a range of specific frequencies.

This makes the term a borderless statistic, but the idea is to evaluate the probability of any event occurring and determine the chances of said probability doing so.

By assuming that a balance must occur, the numbers become enticing to the reader when determining the odds, which is a phenomenon known as *Gambler's Fallacy*.

At its core, the law of averages assumes that an event is due to happen. A common example of the theory can be seen while studying coin toss probabilities, where a coin is equally as likely to land on its head as its tail.

If somebody flips a coin and records a few heads in succession, that person may believe that the following toss is more likely to come up tails than heads to even things out.

However, the genuine probabilities of the two results are still the same for the next coin flip and any that may follow.

The results of previous coin flips don't determine the probability, as each and every coin flip is a free occasion of itself.

For sports fans, consider this example as well. If a player is currently batting at a season average of .250, then they can be expected to hit a baseball 25% of the time it is pitched their way.

However, this number is misleading, as anyone who follows baseball knows that hitters often run into streaks and slumps that can drastically affect their batting averages for days or weeks.

The law of averages then comes into effect during these timespans, as people will evaluate their recent hits and suggest that the player is, in for a miss, or in for a hit, to even out the odds that are implied by the season averages.

According to the stricter law, known as the law of large numbers, no type of estimate of that count can logistically be made.

## The Law of Large Numbers

The law of large numbers is different from the law of averages, and people commonly confuse the two.

While the law of averages does not act as a mathematical principle, the law of large numbers does, invoking probability theory in its process of explanation.

To summarize, the law of numbers is a mathematical theory that predicts the result of an event by performing the same study many times.

By the law's rules, an average of results should be taken from a large number of trials, and these should be close to the average expected value.

The law of large numbers, in theory, guarantees stable long-term results of random events.

For example, while a casino may lose money in a single roulette bet, its earnings will ultimately beat out the loss, as a large number of spins is generally required until a jackpot can be hit.

Consider the law of large numbers as the explanation behind the law of averages, similar to how blockchain is the technology behind cryptocurrency.

Many people use the terms interchangeably, but they are not the same thing at all.

## The Law of Averages and Cryptocurrency

The law of averages, in any case, can apply to any form of investing or monetary option through its use of probability.

In a bullish market, traders will eventually expect a coin's price to continue rising if it has been soaring for a few days, while also making an exception for the ladder by claiming that the coin will eventually rise in price.

The aforementioned Gambler's Fallacy is a common mindset that crypto investors fall into, which often causes them to mismanage their portfolios.

So what about the law of averages is related to cryptocurrency? For starters, the probability odds behind the law of large numbers help investors to determine the price of any coin from five to 10 years from the time of purchase.

This is how many finance websites create estimated valuations for Bitcoin and Ethereum in 2025 when it is currently 2021.

The law of averages and the law of large numbers can help to predict volatility, which is a major price variable in the cryptocurrency market scene.

## Chance Processes

The volatility of cryptocurrencies can be estimated through a method known as the chance process.

Chance processes, also known as stochastic processes, are a collection of random variables that can be used to represent the evolution of valuation over time.

One approach of the chance process involves treating the values as functions whose values are random variables.

These variables have certain probability factors, and although the random values can be independent variables, most of the time change processes consider these as statistical correlations.

Chance processes also determine a mathematical formation of succession known as a random walk and measure the chance process on a collection of functions gathered through the study process.

By evaluating the chance of a price's eventual rise, crypto traders and researchers can determine how much a coin can be worth without worrying about the biases of either bull markets or crashes.

The same evaluation has been done in the stock market as well, with studies reporting accurate valuations for BSE and NSE stocks through a 187-week study report on the stock's valuation.

Although cryptocurrency is volatile, a prediction of its volatility can be used for investors to create investment and trading strategies.

By the rules of the law of averages, a price rise is bound to eventually happen for any coin, and it is only a matter of time before the right numbers line up and hit their valuation.

This lineup of numbers is what predicted the surge of cryptocurrency bull markets in 2017 and 2021, with prices slowly rising to a point of explosion. This event is known as a *bubble*.

During the bubble period, prices will slowly creep up and rise in investors' portfolios, leaving everyone to cross their fingers and hope for a spike in valuation.

Crypto investors and researchers alike will look into the future valuation of all coins using chance processes to determine whether or not a bull market will be in effect soon.

Eventually, the bubble will pop, allowing all cryptocurrency prices to spike at all-time highs, allowing all investors to make exponential profits from their original investments.

The chance process also evaluates when a market will crash, so it is not all fun and games through the law of averages and cryptocurrency.

Typically, however, the crash evaluation goes overlooked, as investors fall in love with the passive income that comes with a popped bubble and a surging marketplace.

Therefore, it is important to remember that all rises must eventually crash and that you should sell when you've made a profit that you're comfortable with.

### Overview

The law of averages, the law of large numbers, and the chance process are all factors in determining a coin's future valuation, which is advantageous for all crypto investors to look into and understand.

Either way, a cryptocurrency investment can take a long time to turn a profit, depending on when the investment is made.

Some traders may get lucky and find themselves investing just before a bubble pops, allowing them to make a great short-term profit.

However, long-term investments are still the way to go for profitability chances. Next, let's take a look at the mechanics of investing and the strategies that come along with them.

## Chapter 9: Playing the Long Game (Buy and Hold)

The original Bitcoin investors saw immense capital gains come their way mainly because they chose to hold their investments until the valuation eventually skyrocketed.

However, buying and holding cryptocurrency shares did not become popular in its early renditions, and instead, people opted to sell and buy again as a method of day trading until they were satisfied.

This took up a significant amount of time, and the same profits could be made by just holding the investment instead. So, what paved the way to allow holding to be a profitable option?

Believe it or not, the entire concept became viable through jokes and misspellings. In 2013, Bitcoin investors discussed the current price drops on an online chat forum.

As most investors mentioned selling before the price crashed, one investor said that they would continue to hold their shares even when the price fell.

He created a post about holding his shares and titled it, *I am hodling,* meaning to write *holding* instead of *hodling*.

The community embraced the misspelling and eventually turned HODLers into a type of crypto investor.

Today, HODL stands for *Hold On for Dear Life*, as a way to express the stress that volatility brings when one is holding an investment.

HODLers are commonly seen today as jokes, especially in online forums that focus on meme coins and other commodities.

They hold their investments with dreams of the coin *going to the moon.*

These investors are seen as the original risky traders; people who were willing to experience losses if it meant an eventual exponential growth.

Their investment mindsets specifically played on the law of averages and the Gambler's Fallacy, where they believed that their losses would eventually even out and become profits.

Whether the market is up, down, sideways, or completely in the red, these investors stick to their original investments, confident in the long-term value of the chosen coins.

## Why Buy and Hold Works

Although holding has a comedic background, the strategy does work.

The investor who held shares in 2013, likely continues to hold today, and they have seen tens of thousands of dollars of profit as a result. So, what made investors take the strategy seriously, and what turned investors from HODLers to holders?

*Buy and hold* is one of the easiest strategy methods to implement in cryptocurrency investing, as it follows these specific steps:

1. Buy a share.
2. Hold a share.

That's all it takes to buy and hold. You don't need to worry about setting up trades, calculating take-profits or stop-losses, or worry about constantly checking your portfolio.

You simply buy, hold, and wait a set amount of time until you check on your investments again.

People who periodically invest in cryptocurrency also don't have to worry about timing the market, which is one of the most difficult and stressful things to do.

Knowing when to buy is crucial, but the price doesn't matter when you're planning to hold a share because buy and hold is a long-term deal.

As long as you aren't buying a coin at a very high valuation point, you can expect to see some form of profit within a few years.

Therefore, you're waiting for a good buy-in opportunity, rather than the best buy-in opportunity.

This eliminates the process of finding a good entry, as nearly any price you pay will result in profitability.

It also helps people who struggle with controlling their stress and emotions at pivotal trading points, such as when crypto is drastically rising or falling in value.

Beginners may find themselves panic-selling, a term that describes a behavior where people constantly resell and rebuy their positions, causing a loss of profit almost instantly as fees are applied to every sale and purchase.

A lack of control of emotions basically constitutes a loss in your portfolio, so the practice of buying a share and holding it for some time eliminates the fear of volatility, and the investment will eventually become an afterthought.

If you're still stressed, remember that the market will eventually turn positive, as per the rules of the law of averages.

The only real downside of buying and holding comes when a market enters a bull run.

This describes a time when a market hits a valuable point, and every crypto coin rises in price.

This can cause the overvaluation of a coin's price, meaning that you may not get the payoff you're looking for from a long-term holding strategy.

Instead, the market will eventually crash, causing you to lose much of your initial investment at the start of your investment period, and the coin may not ultimately reach the same all-time highs again.

If you are entering a bull run with an initial investment already in place, the risks will be minimized, but your investment will need a lot more care.

To manage a buy and hold strategy, set a risk-loss ratio for yourself, and watch the coin's value whenever you can.

If you feel that a coin has hit its highest profitable point, and your research can confirm that, then sell the profit amount and wait until the market falls again.

This gives you additional money to invest on top of your original investment and is useful for bridging the long period of decline that follows a bull run, which is known as a bear market.

Bear markets are prolonged periods of decline and loss in a coin's value, which occurs after the sudden rise that comes with a bull run.

Bear markets are great times to invest and apply the buy and hold strategy, as you get to invest at a low price and wait for another bull run to occur.

In recent years, bull runs have occurred in both 2017 and 2021, so it is safe to say that you could be waiting a few years until you can appreciate a return on your investment.

## Overview

There are comparative advantages between regular crypto trading and holding an investment, and while period investing reduces the risk of volatility, managing market timing is still an incredibly important activity.

The biggest problem beginning crypto investors face is managing a portfolio, and being an investor or trader doesn't mean that you constantly have to check and trade your investments and coins.

It is completely reasonable, and viable, to periodically check on your investments without making any major changes, so don't be too hard on yourself if you don't see a massive profit overnight.

The goal is to play the long game for a few years, to see a viable return on your investment as a result.

For experienced traders, period investing may not be as enticing as other options, as experienced traders look for the most hands-on and short-term forms of investing.

Overall, if you aren't comfortable in your ability to trade, but still want to invest, simply buy into a coin and hold it until you gain your profit.

Be sure to budget your investment with the previous information discussed, and don't take on more risk than necessary.

## Chapter 10: Where to Buy Cryptocurrency

It is time for you to finally make your first crypto investment.

However, you still have to choose a platform to buy on, as well as figure out which platform is best for you.

So where do you buy cryptocurrency, and how should it be stored?

This chapter will explain a lot of new and enticing concepts, such as buying crypto, storing crypto, the pros and cons of exchanges, the best exchanges for certain coins, and crypto-security options.

If you find yourself struggling to keep up, take your time and read through everything as thoroughly as you can

## How to Buy Crypto

Buying crypto can be broken down into a simple four-step process:

1. Choosing a crypto exchange

Most cryptocurrencies are available on digital exchanges, which are online marketplaces that allow users to trade, sell, and buy shares.

This means that to buy a cryptocurrency, you're going to need to commit to an exchange to use. For organization's sake, you don't want to use more than two crypto exchanges, but things can change depending on a coin's availability.

There are hundreds of crypto exchanges on the market, which can make the choosing process difficult, however, it is always important to remember that when choosing an exchange, you should look for ones that balance the ease of use between low fees and high security.

In other words, be sure that your transactions aren't being charged a hefty service fee, and be confident that the exchange's security system is airtight by looking at user reviews to ensure that proper blockchain protocol is taking place.

All of these are signs that the exchange is reliable, and isn't trying to hustle you out of any money you've deposited for an investment.

The advisable top picks would be Coinbase, Gemini, and Binance, but we'll expand on those later.

For now, let's enter step two of buying a cryptocurrency.

2. Decide on a payment option

To use an exchange, you must deposit funds into your account. You can do this through several available options, including:

- bank transfers
- PayPal
- wire transfers
- cryptocurrency wallets
- credit and debit cards

Keep in mind that some platforms have different fees for different depositing options.

For example, Coinbase doesn't charge a fee for bank transfers, but it does charge $10 on wire transfers and 2.5% on PayPal transactions.

3. Place an order

Once your account is funded, you can buy your first order of Bitcoin or any other coin for that matter.

The markets all have options and charts to go along with every cryptocurrency, so you can focus on finding a good buying time to choose your investment.

Depending on the platform you use, buying can be as simple as pressing a button, or you may have to enter Bitcoin's ticker symbol, BTC, into the search engine to find it.

Regardless, buying a coin is as simple as it sounds. Simply enter the amount you want to invest, and wait until your purchase is confirmed.

4. Select a safe storage option

Now that you've bought your coin of choice, your investment has been made, and it is viewable in the wallet section of your exchange.

This acts as a form of storage for your crypto investment, and although it is relatively safe, some people are fearful of online hackers and data breaches.

If you wish, you can export your funds to a hard wallet, and only send them back when the market gives you a chance to sell.

## Best Crypto Exchange Options

Here, we'll discuss some crypto exchange options for general traders and beginners, as well as options for altcoins and DeFi exchanges.

### For Beginners

Coinbase and Coinbase Pro are two relatively popular options for all kinds of traders, as the platform is based on simplicity.

Fees are typically low as well, ranging from US$0.99 to US$2.99 depending on the dollar value of the purchase.

There are plenty of altcoin options as well, and the interface is incredibly easy to use and get adjusted to.

Coinbase, as a company, is very high in liquidation, meaning that they are in good financial health, which is what you want to know about the exchange you're depositing your funds into.

That's not to say that the platform is perfect, as there are some negatives to the platform. Fees are higher when you use the free version of the platform, so upgrading to Coinbase Pro is essential.

Security is also a concern; although it is tight, the user does not control wallet keys. This means that if a hacker gets hold of your account information, there is no protocol in place to stop any sudden large transactions.

The good news is that Coinbase is one of the few platforms that has managed to avoid controversy by always being cautious of fraud coins and shady practices.

In general, Coinbase is an easy-to-use exchange that lowers the barrier to entry for cryptocurrency investing.

Another good beginner exchange is Cash App, which is useful for getting introduced to cryptocurrency, but there isn't much else to it.

Similar to platforms like Venmo, Cash App is a peer-to-peer money transfer system that allows users to pay rent to roommates, split food, or shop online.

Recently, the platform has allowed for Bitcoin to be used as a deposit and withdrawal option, technically making the platform an exchange.

The user interface is very simple, and it allows Bitcoin to work under its main gimmick; fast peer-to-peer transfers.

However, the degree to which Cash App can be considered as an exchange is heavily limited.

The only coin currently available is Bitcoin, and there's a 3% fee when sending money linked via credit card.

Additionally, the withdrawal limit of Bitcoin is US$2,000 a day and US$5,000 a week, which is incredibly low, by investment standards.

For beginners, this option is good, but you will do well to switch to a more refined exchange after you get comfortable.

**For Altcoins**

For investing in altcoins and other options outside of Bitcoin, Binance is the way to go. The platform's fees are incredibly small, with a 0.1% charge for both takers and makers.

This can scale down to 0.02% with trade volume, thanks to the platform's own cryptocurrency, BNB, which helps to lower fees by 25%.

The low fees are a great advantage of the platform, giving Binance a wide variety of coins in which to invest, as well as an advanced charting system to go along with it.

The downside is that Binance is typically geared towards advanced users, and even if you choose to use the simplified Binance Lite, you may still run into issues.

The platform has fewer trading pairs than its counterparts, as well as limited depositing options. For users outside the US, depositing and withdrawing funds can be a very tedious process.

Seventeen US states, including New York and Texas, also don't support the exchange, so accessibility is a big issue for the platform.

Even so, Binance is a great platform with over 100 trading pairs to choose from. Its low fees and simple interface make it the best platform to trade and sell altcoins on, even if the withdrawal method is messy.

**Best Decentralized Exchange**

The best-decentralized exchange available right now is Bisq, which works to improve on issues that other exchanges find themselves having.

For starters, fees are incredibly low, and they are charged as taxes on the crypto sent. For example, when paying fees using Bitcoin, the cost to trade is set at 0.1% on the maker side and 0.7% on the taker side.

This means that there are no fees on your initial deposit, which usually occurs on most other exchanges, and you get to use the full amount you want to invest.

Additionally, being decentralized is a positive adjustment in cryptocurrency, as are the 25 available payment options that can be used.

There are also mobile renditions of the app available for both Android and iOS, making the exchange easily accessible.

The downside comes with the slow transaction speeds and low trading volumes, due to the exchange being less popular than other mainstream options, like Binance and Coinbase.

This is mainly because the platform wasn't designed for active trading, but rather, it was made as a casual alternative for exchange markets that are very accessible via blockchain technology.

Many would argue that this form of accessibility opens up possibilities for criminal activity, and it also grants units of accounts to people in countries with less-developed banking systems and institutions.

Bitcoin, when used in tandem with an exchange like Bisq, can be a good solution to these issues.

## Recognizing a Secure Exchange

Although cryptocurrency likes to praise itself as the most secure form of digital investing, exchanges are susceptible to hacks and breaches.

On average, exchanges lose US$2.7 million daily, with the figure set to increase in the future.

Hacking attacks are becoming more elaborate, and exchanges are not as secure as other deposit options.

These breaches and hacks, as well as regular security risks, are simple reasons why you need to be able to recognize a secure exchange.

There is no guarantee that you won't be a victim of statistics, as the best and most reliable platforms are typically open about the level of security they provide.

Most exchanges also use 2-step verification processes as an additional form of security, making it harder for hackers to get in.

Even so, you can have your data breached at any time, albeit unlikely, using an exchange.

There are two things you can look for when determining a secure exchange to use for your investment.

## HTTPS

HTTPS is an authentication and security protocol completely implemented in browsers and web servers. Secure exchanges have a valid HTTPS certificate, and browsers like Google Chrome and Firefox typically confirm it by displaying an image of a lock in the address bar.

This indicates that the site is safe and secure to an acceptable level.

It stands for Hypertext Transfer Protocol Secure and is completely different from HTTP, which stands for Hypertext Transfer Protocol.

HTTPS confirms a website's security using protocols like Transport Layer Security (TLS) or Secure Sockets Layer (SSL) to encrypt any data deemed sensitive, prevent the alteration of data during data transfers, and authenticate users to use the website.

On the other hand, HTTP is simply an online address. HTTP has no actual ability to implement security, as HTTP websites often consist of insecure systems that may steal people's data upon access.

That isn't to say all HTTP websites are suspect, but it is advisable to invest in exchanges where HTTPS is used in the address of the website instead.

**Secure Passwords**

Good exchanges don't allow you to use weak passwords and measure the strength of your password with a meter next to the account creation screen.

According to the legend, red is weak, yellow is acceptable, and green is good for security. A secure password usually consists of a mix of regular and capital letters, symbols, and numbers, suggesting that it would take longer for a computer program to guess your password.

A 2-step verification, also known as Two-Factor Authentication (2FA), is critical, as it forces any login attempt to go to another device for verification.

This ensures that, even if your account is breached by hackers, they won't be able to log in without your consent and agreement.

## *Overview*

It is best to compare options and consider your form of investment strategy when choosing an exchange. For continuous trading, exchanges like Binance would be optimal.

As for buying and holding options, Bisq is a secure, low-volume option. If you're still anxious about hacks and stolen funds, don't stress.

After all, even if your security is breached, there's not much to worry about.

Nearly all exchanges have some form of funds insurance that protects investors in the event of a hack.

The platform reimburses investors and pays for the damages out of its own pocket, so your investment will always be paid back in full.

And now, you have the necessary knowledge to successfully choose and use a crypto exchange.

It is important to reiterate that, at the time of writing, banks and other financial third parties have banned transactions to cryptocurrency exchanges.

Be cautious when investing, and find something that suits your needs to the fullest extent possible.

## Chapter 11: Choosing a Coin to Invest In

Now that you are comfortable with an exchange and have made an initial deposit, it is time to invest in a cryptocurrency of your choice.

Similar to choosing a stock to invest in, you will want to find something that suits your needs and goals while also diversifying your portfolio.

Because of the volatile market system, it is better to invest in multiple coins with your budget rather than invest in one and put all your cards (or in this case, coins) on the table.

With that being said, how exactly would you know which coins to invest in?

Before we introduce you to the methods of choosing a crypto investment, let's reiterate a concept that you must always go back to when it comes to investing:

**Only invest as much as you can afford to lose**

Cryptocurrency investments are useful, but if there comes a time when you might need money, you could find yourself looking at your investment portfolio and wishing that you had never invested it.

Investment accounts should not be touched or have money taken out of them in most circumstances, so if a lack of money could pose a potential problem down the line, consider adjusting your budget accordingly.

Finding a proper buy-in time is also an important part of the process. In 2017, for example, many were enticed to buy into Bitcoin when it was worth roughly US$20,000, only for it to fall within hours, causing investors to lose thousands of dollars in a few hours and sell within the same time frame.

Additionally, if they had only waited a week to invest, they would have seen massive profits. Finding a buy-in time, and managing your portfolio, are both essential elements of successful cryptocurrency investing.

## The 10 Ways of Choosing a Crypto Investment

There are 10 things you should look into, as a crypto investor, when choosing a coin for investing, which are:

1. The community

A big part of the cryptocurrency scene is the community, with online communities dedicated to their favorite coins.

Look out for cryptocurrencies with a strong following behind them, as well as look into the profiles of the community members themselves.

Meme coin communities tend to be more humorous and carefree, while serious investing communities will focus more on statistics and numbers.

Regardless of the type of community you choose, as long as it has a strong following, a strong community means a better chance of profit.

2. Analysis

Analyzing a coin involves looking into every aspect of what makes the coin viable. This can be anything that increases the valuation, including the team behind the coin, their ambitions, strengths, weaknesses, etc.

If you are new to the crypto scene, do not let the technical side of things scare you away. A simple search into a coin's history and price value is more than enough to help.

### 3. Teams

Researching and understanding the teams behind the coins are important tasks for a successful investor.

Consider who the person behind the crypto is, their background in the crypto marketplace and if they have a proven history of success.

All of this information can help to determine if you are investing in a reliable coin or a fraudulent scam.

Note that most exchanges do not accept risky coins that may seem fraudulent, so this shouldn't be a worry unless you are investing without an exchange. Always do your research.

### 4. Technology

We touched on the technology behind cryptocurrency for a reason, that being that understanding how a coin has been developed and is used will effectively benefit you when it comes to investing.

You have to be able to understand how it will perform against the competition, and what makes it stand out from the crowd.

Examine big innovators and their methods, and look into what else they are working on.

Fork coins based on Bitcoin and Ethereum, such as Litecoin and Ethereum Classic, are good options for this exact reason.

Without understanding the technology of the two, you would have no reason to invest in them at all.

You now understand that, like forks, their valuation follows the same market correlation at a lower investment price than the originals.

5. White paper

Bitcoin is not the only crypto with a white paper; nearly every cryptocurrency has published a white paper along with its release.

These documents outline the purpose of the coins, their technology, how they work, and their overall visions (which are discussed next).

Consider a coin's white paper as a brochure guide to everything about it, and consider studying it as a way of investigating a coin's investment potential.

## 6. Their vision

The vision of the cryptocurrency is important because it details the plan behind it.

Ideally, a coin should be available for the next 5 to 10 years to make the most of an investment, and if the coin doesn't exist long-term, then there isn't a point in creating it.

It's okay to have a big vision, as a big vision usually indicates an ambitious founder behind it, but if there isn't a clear plan behind it as well, the coin will inevitably suffer.

## 7. Their leadership

Leaders are often the founders of the coin, and in some cases, the ones in charge of development.

By understanding who they are, and researching their previous projects and endeavors, you can understand how they work with a team.

These are the people who carry out the vision, so if the team behind the project is reported to be unhappy, they may not be the one you're looking for.

## 8. Pricing history

The present will eventually repeat the past, according to the law of averages, and evaluating the pricing history of a coin will help you to understand how it fluctuates.

Not only should the volatility be examined, but its resilience related to crashes and price evaluations should be looked into as well.

Coin Ranking is a good website to look at for these numbers. Interactive Crypto and Coinigy are good options for online research as well.

## 9. Credibility and reputation

A crypto's credibility and reputation are massively important to your investment because, if a coin isn't reliable, you would be taking on a lot of unnecessary risks by investing in it.

Investigating these factors will help you to avoid scams and fraud coins that advertise themselves as short-term startups.

Look through crypto communities to see if the coin is liked, and if it isn't, look elsewhere for investment options.

10. The road map

The *road map* refers to the future of the coin, or specifically, a development plan laid out by the main team behind the coin.

Check for clear timelines detailed by the development team, as well as scheduled major updates and projected coin limits, as the process goes forward.

**Overview**

Now that you understand what to look for in a coin, you can confidently choose an investment.

What to choose, however, is a different story entirely.

The following chapter will discuss the role of Bitcoin and others in investment plans, as well as other ways of obtaining cryptocurrencies without initial investments.

The 10-step guide above is to be used as a checklist of sorts, and before you decide on a coin, remember that the most important deciding factor regarding investment in a coin is how you feel about it.

If you aren't comfortable with your choice or are unsure of whether this is the best choice for you, don't get ahead of yourself.

Reevaluate accordingly to the options around you.

## Chapter 12: Are There Better Bets than Bitcoin?

Throughout this guide, we've introduced a multitude of alternatives to Bitcoin. This chapter will expand on why there are better options than the traditional Bitcoin blockchain.

To expand on this topic, however, let's talk about the cons that investors may face when choosing Bitcoin as their investment of choice.

First, we must understand why Bitcoin investors may sometimes find themselves losing money, rather than appreciating returns on their investments.

To begin, let's talk numbers. At the moment of writing, Bitcoin is valued at around US$40,000, meaning that, to own a share of the coin, you would have to make an initial deposit of US$40,000.

That is a lot of money to bet on a coin, and likely, only seasoned investors would qualify in this category. For smaller and beginner investors, however, they would be ill-advised to make a deposit of this size.

Granted, you can buy portions of a share when investing in crypto, but your potential value would be ruined by the math behind the coin.

For example, say you invest US$5,000 in Bitcoin, which would represent approximately 0.125 BTC.

If Bitcoin were to skyrocket in valuation and hit US$100,000, then your portfolio would be boosted by 150%, and your Bitcoin shares would then be worth $7,500.

It is a great return, however, you would make a lot less than someone who owned an entire share, to begin with, as they would see the same portfolio boost, but gain US$60,000 more in their account.

The inability of investors to own full shares without large down payments is a hindrance to the coin's overall ability to adjust to the current cryptocurrency world, and it shows with its current valuation.

Let's also consider the technology behind Bitcoin, and the company's stubbornness to adapt to today's cryptocurrency world.

A fork coin was created in the process of enhancing security, which is a great sign of change, yet Bitcoin's competitors continue to readjust and revamp their systems in ways that have never been seen before.

Somehow, Bitcoin's technology fails to compete with many variants of altcoins worth 100 times less than Bitcoin's value.

How exactly is Bitcoin, a coin currently priced at US$40,000, failing to keep up with other technologies with larger budgets and more room for failure?

Due to these issues, investing in Bitcoin may not be the move you're looking for, so you may consider investing in a different option, which would make sense if you're worried about Bitcoin's future.

**The Potential of Ethereum**

In terms of the long run, Ethereum has constantly proven to be a consistent and more reliable investment than Bitcoin, for a multitude of reasons.

To understand why this is, let's consider the coin's future valuation. In early March of 2021, ETH reached an all-time high of US$4,000 and slowly dropped back down to US$1,950.

It may seem like a downgrade, however, the current market is recovering from the previous bull run, and is currently taking a bearish stance.

This makes it a great time to invest in Ethereum for the long term, as the price is low enough to accommodate owning multiple shares, meaning that you would be making the best you can out of your investment.

Let's apply the same Bitcoin numbers to Ethereum to see if the overall return on investment is the same.

If you were to invest US$5000 into the current ETH shares, you would own 2.56 ETH; a fair amount, considering the same investment in Bitcoin would earn you 0.125 BTC.

Now, let's say that you plan to sell Ethereum during the next bull run, where it could potentially see a price valuation of US$7,000.

Your initial investment of US$5,000 would then net you a profit of US$12,928, which is a portfolio boost of 256%.

Notice how owning a share actually pays out more than owning a portion of a share, and Ethereum lives up to that standard while Bitcoin is submerged by better options.

Also, consider the technology behind Ethereum—that being the Augur platform.

The Augur platform, more simply known as Augur, is Ethereum's product that acts as a solution to Bitcoin's essential problems.

The exchange works as a decentralized prediction market and is one of the biggest decentralized apps on the Ethereum database.

So long as Augur doesn't slow the main system down, the project will be a positive for Ethereum, as they will have successfully created a landscape that allows investments, bets, and other forms of monetary exchange to take place directly through the ETH coin and Ethereum's own technology.

This only adds another point that gives Ethereum credibility—their expansion as a company.

Ethereum continues to promote itself as a platform to create investment opportunities for, instead of simply being a company to invest in.

This led to developers being enticed by the simple-to-use code, and the cryptocurrency scene evolved because of this technology.

Bitcoin, however, has not expanded outside of its forks, such as Litecoin and Bitcoin Classic.

Bitcoin is ahead in valuation, but Ethereum is slowly catching up in the grand scheme of things by simply implementing and promoting new ideas.

The leaders are truly ambitious with a game plan that supports them, which makes it an enticing coin to invest your money in.

Finally, let's discuss software mining—Ethereum's counter play to traditional mining—and the problems that occur with it.

We'll expand on mining in the next chapter, but for now, all you need to know is that mining is a power-hungry process that allows users to utilize computer power for the earning of cryptocurrency.

Energy consumption has been a heavily criticized feature of the process, however, Ethereum's introduction of proof of stake technology created an alternative to traditional mining methods.

This was likely done to tackle the criticism of Bitcoin as a company, and software mining continues to be a relevant feature that investors and traders alike use to make additional profit on their deposits.

Overall, Ethereum's control over the marketplace and its technology make it a more enticing investment than Bitcoin, and although the two are far apart in terms of valuation, Ethereum is slowly closing the popularity and technical gaps between the two competing companies.

**Overview**

The goal of this chapter wasn't to show that Bitcoin is outclassed by its peers, or that Ethereum is the next best thing.

The main concept behind this discussion is to help you to understand that Bitcoin is not the only available option.

If you believe in Bitcoin, but don't have the funds to own a share, invest in fork coins such as Litecoin and Bitcoin Classic that follow Bitcoin's fluctuation and price changes.

The same goes for Ethereum and their forks as well, and it is important to have a diverse portfolio when investing in any market, for that matter.

Due to the volatility of crypto, it is best to invest in multiple coins rather than sticking with one and hoping for the best.

Expand your available options and look into everything you possibly can before making an investment choice, and understand that at times, there are better options than the mainstream choices.

# Chapter 13: What About Mining?

You may have heard of a process known as crypto mining, which can help investors to gain cryptocurrencies without an initial deposit to an exchange.

This is an incredible advantage to have over competing investors, however, the process can be confusing to understand.

Use this chapter as a guide to all things related to mining, and use the information to choose whether or not to invest in the mining process.

To begin, let's break down what mining is and where it originated from. Crypto mining, or more specifically Bitcoin mining, is the process by which new Bitcoins are entered into circulation.

This is done through hardware or software that allows the process to occur, which varies in cost, depending on the product's mining capabilities and specifications.

The process involves computers that solve difficult math problems to determine whether or not a coin can be taken out of circulation, and the reward is cryptocurrency in your hard wallet.

In other words, miners receive cryptocurrency as a reward for completing *blocks* of verified transactions, which are added to the entire blockchain.

This allows for coins to stay in circulation for longer than expected, giving the coin an increased future valuation.

What's important to understand is how mining rewards are paid out.

In cryptocurrency networks, users are often trying to solve puzzles involving nonces and hashes (which we will touch on later in this chapter), as they aim for a target under the predefined conditions of the blockchain.

From there, the miner verifies transactions by solving these same puzzles, and adding the new block to the blockchain as it is verified by other users.

Then, the Bitcoins associated with the transactions can be spent and the transfer between users can be made.

For completing these puzzles, miners are rewarded with *6.25 BTC*. For comparison, as of today, that would be worth around US$207,000, all for solving a puzzle.

Generating a value called hash is also a crucial part of the process, and to generate it, miners use an SHA-256 hashing algorithm and then determine the hash value.

Don't worry about the complicated algorithm name. Instead, you should be focusing on the generation of the value.

The more that value can be generated, the faster the puzzle can be solved, which means a faster Bitcoin reward.

Before continuing into the different types of mining methods, let's break things down into an example, to simplify the information:

Say you wish to send a share of Bitcoin to a friend. The first step of the process would involve the transaction data, as it sits in an unmined pool of transactions.

Bitcoin miners work to validate the transaction using a process known as proof of work, and the miner who validates it first shares the results with other various forms of data.

After that data is verified, the block can work to get verified, and once the block is verified, it can enter the blockchain.

The miner who verifies it gains their reward, and the transaction can take place for exchange and transfer usage.

## Different Types of Miners

Different types of mining methods vary, depending on your computer's hardware specifications, which is why most miners have invested in a mining rig—a combination of hardware that generates computing power at a greater scale than with a piece of standalone equipment.

This is because the directed acyclic graph (DAG) is an algorithm that requires a lot of power for it to be solved properly.

The DAG increases in power over time and video cards need a lot of memory to be able to process the values.

There are currently three different ways of mining cryptocurrency; however, only two are viable for profit today. A lot of these methods are also connected with mining rigs that use these components to mine more efficiently.

Mining rigs are essentially computers that allow for additional GPUs to be implemented into the motherboard, and you don't need an extensive computer background to build one yourself. These methods are:

1.  ASIC mining: Bitcoin

ASIC stands for an application-specific integrated circuit, and these circuits are designed for a specific purpose. In this case, ASIC miners refer to devices that are purposely made with the intention of mining cryptocurrency.

Generally, each ASIC miner is constructed to mine certain crypto (i.e., Bitcoin ASIC miners can only mine Bitcoin), as the hardware is optimized to solve the mining algorithm and crack the puzzles that follow it.

In the beginning stages of crypto mining, ASIC miners were only capable of mining Bitcoin. This is due to the double SHA-256 hash, which is an iteration of the Bitcoin algorithm.

The double SHA-256 hash is currently at odds with normal Bitcoin mining, as its method of checking and verifying transactions tends to work against each other.

This is why many altcoins, such as Litecoin, use the SCRYPT algorithm, which can process bigger memory volumes and larger hash values than the double SHA-256 hash.

There are ASIC miners with SCRYPT algorithms available, such as the AntMiner L3++, that allow for SCRYPT to take place and be effective. It is also important to note that ASIC miners are faster than GPU miners, with the drawback being the cost.

A good ASIC miner costs a few thousand dollars, and you'll have to buy a few of those with the proper attachments for it to be cost-effective.

## 2. GPU mining: Altcoins

GPU mining became a popular alternative to ASIC mining after Bitcoin's bull run in 2017.

This process involves sending all the mining power to a computer's GPU, which is a computer's video card, and the extra power is used to theoretically allow investors to mine cryptocurrencies from their laptops or home computers.

However, it is still better to invest in a mining rig, as you run the risk of damaging your computer with the intense power usage.

You'll need hardware that can mine cryptocurrency without the risk of overheating, meaning that you need to know what kind of GPU miners are best to complete the process.

The most popular GPU miners use today are Nvidia cards and AMD cards. The difference between the two lies in the API model that gives it additional power; Nvidia uses CUDA, which harnesses the GPUs power, and AMD uses openCL, which recently saw a revamped update with openCL 2.0.

Most modern GPUs have the necessary drivers available for download on their websites, as technology advances with updates coming at a constant rate.

It is important to note that GPU miners are not used to mine Bitcoin, but rather they are used to mine altcoins that are just as profitable.

The problem today is that more power is needed to mine a cryptocurrency, as well as the rewards halving almost every few years, due to a lack of supply.

Before 2020, only about 4GB of GPU computing power was needed for a miner to function properly.

In recent years, however, the standards of technology have changed, and most mining rigs require 8GBs of computing power or more, which is double the amount of power needed in previous years.

Using multiple GPUs with one motherboard allows you to save money that can be invested in extra GPUs.

It is still possible to mine a variance of altcoins with 4GB of power, but if you're looking to mine Ethereum, you're going to have to double down to power it.

Due to the power demand, miners came up with a collaborative solution, creating operations that combine power between users.

These are known as GPU mining operations, which take place in a shared pool so miners combine their computing powers into a big group that can generate solutions more efficiently.

Rewards are still handed out to all parties, but they are split based on how much power they contribute. If you were to mine solo, all the rewards would go directly to you.

3. CPU mining

A CPU is like a computer's brain, as it controls the operations of all parts.

Thus, CPU mining involves sending all the power to the computer's CPU.

This used to be viable because CPUs perform all types of data processing that makes crypto mining a lot easier, but with the heavier competition, blockchains moved away to more favorable options.

It's still possible to mine with a CPU using programs like Loki and Nimiq, and the time spent to get it to run correctly may payback on your initial investment.

A major issue with CPU mining, however, is overheating, as only so much power can be sent to a CPU to maintain itself.

The processors within the CPU are what make mining possible, as it has enough components to conduct calculations on the algorithmic puzzles.

Most computers use a dual-core CPU, which allows for double the power to be administered to the hardware, and this alone is enough to power a mining rig.

The only thing your CPU should do with the miner is start it up, and the kind of CPU you need is dependent on the motherboard you have.

Expensive options, like the AMD Ryzen 7 or the AMD Ryzen 9, are also available (which will take an AMD motherboard like the ASUS ROG STRIX), but you should focus that budget on obtaining more GPUs.

The goal should be to invest your budget into GPUs, allowing you to cut some costs on your mining rig by going for a lower-end CPU.

Most mining rigs are connected to a motherboard that takes nearly all of the above and connects them together. For those interested in the mining process, but who don't want to use a pool, we've compiled a list of reliable mining software that does the job just as well for solo mining. This list includes:

- CGMiner
- BFGMiner
- MultiMiner
- Awesome Miner

This is a good time to mention that mining does not just apply to Bitcoin.

In fact, plenty of altcoins can be mined using the same methods listed above, and depending on the construction of the blockchain, different amounts of power can be expected when mining certain altcoins.

Even meme coins have a mining community behind them, with DOGE investors using software miners to scalp out the infinite supply of DOGE being thrown into the market every day.

If you find a coin you wish to mine, then look into how much power it'll take to run the miner properly. From there, all you need to understand is how hash functions play a part in the mining process.

Take a look at https://whattomine.com/coins? For an example of what coins you can mine with your miner and the estimated profits per day.

### *Hash and How It Works*

Hash, by definition, is a mathematical function that converts an input of length into an encrypted output. To simplify, it is a string of characters that is minimized into a value that best represents the original.

Hash is a fundamental core of the mining process, as hash power can be bought for mining services that require it.

Hash power, on the other hand, refers to the power a mining rig has over the cryptocurrency network.

Power can be bought by renting mining rigs, making a commitment to cloud mining contracts, or by ordering hash power from websites such as NiceHash.

Hash works by taking the inputs of a variable and returning them to fixed outputs.

This follows the same technology that cryptography does, as the message of data is passed through hash functions while applying security properties.

The functions are commonly used in computing tasks, such as security while authenticating information.

If this sounds similar to Chapter 2's introduction to blockchain, then you're starting to understand why hash is important.

Hash works with cryptography and is an essential part of making crypto transactions secure. Miners also need hash to solve their blockchain puzzles and use hash power to accomplish that goal.

While they are considered weak due to their solvability time, it isn't an easy process at all.

Hash functions add security features when it comes to cryptocurrency mining, making it more difficult to detect the contents of the message or information about both transaction parties.

This makes solving the puzzle a lot harder, but the data time that it takes to complete the process makes the negatives even themselves out. Miners still receive the same reward they typically would, and the only thing that changes is the process.

**Overview**

If you know about computers, data, or arithmetic math, then crypto mining may be a route you choose to take to generate some additional revenue.

Otherwise, this option can be a tedious process for newcomers who don't understand the math behind the mine.

Additionally, the U.S. government is questioning the environmental status of Bitcoin mining, as mining takes up a significant amount of power to generate rewards at a consistent rate.

Be advised that your electricity bill would likely skyrocket, but you would be able to pay it off with your $200,000 Bitcoin reward.

# Chapter 14: Proof of Work

The previous chapter touched upon crypto mining, and how a function known as proof of work can help to make the mining process go faster.

It also enhances security features, avoids fraud issues, and is an important concept to understand when detailing the original Bitcoin white paper and the goals it set out to accomplish.

Today, popular coins such as Bitcoin, Ethereum, and Monero all use the system as a security measure to combat hackers.

In short, proof of work is needed to make online currency work without a third party attached to the process.

So, what is proof of work, how does it work, and how is it applied to everyday cryptocurrency transactions?

## What is Proof of Work?

By definition, proof of work is an algorithm that secures many cryptocurrencies and is a prominent feature in the cryptography of Bitcoin and Ethereum.

It was originally created by Satoshi Nakamoto, Bitcoin's founder, to get it off the ground and allow it to gain popularity.

Although most digital currencies have a central party keeping track of every user and how much they have, proof of work eliminates the central party and works as a virtual assistant to the security measures that cryptocurrency requires to remain nearly unbreachable.

Not only does proof of work enhance security, but it also introduces a counter to double-spending, which is tough to work out without a leader in charge.

Double-spending, as previously mentioned, is an issue where online transactions are replicated, causing a double amount of funds to appear when only half of them are available.

This can lead to over-budgeting, over-evaluation, and most, unfortunately, over-investing.

Proof of work solves this problem by applying cryptographic methods to the blockchain network that inevitably entice every transaction back to the block of data, allowing for funds to be accurately sent without the risk of repetition.

In general, proof of work is the concept behind the Bitcoin white paper's cryptographic solution to third-party interference, so understanding how it works is a necessity for investors and researchers, as well as to cryptocurrency's evolution as a whole.

## How Does It Work?

The example of Bitcoin mining in Chapter 13 sums this process up, except it leaves out the technological aspect of how the process works.

For starters, everything about proof of work is related to blockchain technology and is a necessary part of adding new data to the network.

As blocks are summoned by miners, they are also executing the proof of work system.

This happens because a block is only accepted by the network when a miner comes up with a new winning solution to the blockchain puzzle, which happens about every 10 minutes or so.

Finding the winning answer, however, is difficult because the number of power miners required to solve these puzzles is exponentially high, and the bar is constantly rising.

The rise in power also causes some issues in the blockchain process, and that's where proof of work comes into play.

Its goal is to prevent users from creating extra coins they didn't earn, or double-spending earnings they never obtained in the first place.

With most digital currencies, a third party, such as a bank, keeps track of how much money each person has to combat this issue.

However, cryptocurrency does not have a third party in charge, so proof of work acts as the middleman in all transactions.

To summarize, proof of work creates an opportunity for cryptocurrency to work without a single entity in charge of the operation, making the system entirely peer-to-peer based.

Proof of work technology is also why mining, and especially Bitcoin mining, is a high-energy process.

It was reported that Bitcoin mining uses as much energy as nearly all of the electricity users in Switzerland.

It also doesn't help that three large Bitcoin mining pools take up over half of the current mining regime, making the cryptocurrency mining scene incredibly centralized along the way.

That's a major downgrade from what Bitcoin originally sought out to be, which is a decentralized platform.

Although this is seen as an immense drawback and is a source of much criticism for Bitcoin as a crypto investment, there is a good reason for it.

The more power being poured into securing Bitcoin transactions, the more obstacles a hacker or data breacher needs to tackle before cracking the blockchain's code and functions.

The only plausible way that proof of work can be beaten is if one mining entity can surpass around 51% of Bitcoin's hash rate, which is a difficult thing to do with just one entity.

However, if that does happen, the rules can be temporarily dropped, allowing for double-spending and transaction blocks to occur in the system.

Proof of work, at its core, is a security measure that uses its power sources to battle any who try to take something for themselves.

The monetary reward is incentive enough to ensure that miners follow the rules of proof of work and avoid double-spending their funds.

There is also a protocol in place for times when a miner does break the rules.

For example, if someone submits a solution to the puzzle, but breaks the rules within the block, the rest of the network will reject that block, ultimately leading to a loss of the reward.

That threat alone is enough to keep miners honest, and although it isn't enough to ensure honesty 100% of the time, the blockchain network does a good enough job of making sure that nothing gets compromised.

**Overview**

In a perfect world, cryptocurrency mining and proof of work measures wouldn't be necessary to expand the use of cryptocurrency on a global digital scale.

However, security measures must be taken to secure people's accounts, funds, and other various investments that they risk their portfolios or their hard-earned money on.

Proof of work is heavily integrated into blockchain technology, as well as being a major benefactor to major security enhancements and mining evolutions in the cryptocurrency scene.

Additionally, the system in place is rewarding for miners all over the world, even with its controversial drawbacks.

These flaws are not exactly the fault of the proof of work system, but rather they are a result of eliminating the third party in monetary transactions.

The original Bitcoin white paper set out to create a digital platform where money can be exchanged without a bank overseeing everything, which is why proof of work is essential for the process to develop and function correctly.

Without it, there would be no security, no resistance to data breaches, and ultimately as a result, there would be no Bitcoin (or any other form of cryptocurrency that currently exists).

There are alternatives to the proof of work concept; however, none compare to the protection and security that proof of work brings to the table.

# Chapter 15: Proof of Stake

An alternative method to proof of work is proof of stake, which is a method that maintains the integrity of a cryptocurrency.

This allows for the same security measures to take place without the troublesome issues that proof of work brings to the blockchain network.

The design was first planned out by Ethereum, who succeeded in making the platform more scalable by reducing the energy consumption of the network.

Since then, the platform has seen incredible success, and it is undeniable that the implementation of proof of stake helped Ethereum to reach new heights.

Proof of stake was primarily used in Ethereum 2.0, which involved upgrades that transitioned the platform away from proof of work.

It was implemented in December of 2020 and has seen consistent updates and improvements since its inception. Although it was implemented late last year, the Ethereum creator has been pushing the idea since Ethereum's original white paper in 2013.

Before we get into proof of stake and what it is, we should touch on why proof of anything is needed.

To reiterate a point from the previous chapter, these measures are placed to avoid consensus, which is the act of double-spending.

Without a centralized third party, this can be difficult to accomplish, and it's especially tricky in a peer-to-peer system where thousands of people run the software every day.

This can make it difficult for users to agree with each other; however, with proof of work and proof of stake, a centralized party can be created through the system with cryptography and security enhancements.

**What Is Proof of Stake?**

With proof of stake in place, people can mine blocks based on the amount they hold. For the method to work, however, Ethereum implemented special entities known as *validators*, which are used to select the next blocks entering the blockchain network. Validators are a proof of stakes rendition of cryptocurrency miners, and they tend to tie up some of their own ETH to prevent any loss or penalty in the process.

Considering that validators are the equivalent of miners, rewards are given out for taking part in the proof of stake process. These are awarded for several reasons, including:

- They can attest to a new block, confirm it to be accurate, and follow the rules.
- They win a block through typical mining methods.

To ensure the legitimacy of this process, proof of stake dishes out penalties to those breaking the rules, which can be anything such as:

- If a validator ensures that a block is legitimate with a false transaction or false data history, a portion of the validator's staked resources are taken as a penalty, and furthermore, the user is eventually banned from the network.
- Similar penalties are given if the validator goes offline during the process.

In the Ethereum 2.0 model, validators need to stake about 32 ETH to run a node.

This ensures the security of validators and their willingness to participate in the proof of stake process, and the penalty system also works to ensure that validators don't cheat anyone out of their money.

It also works on a structure of compensation, meaning that validators would not be at an advantage if a data breach or hack occurs in the blockchain system.

**Proof of Work Versus Proof of Stake**

When comparing proof of work to proof of stake, the first question you need to ask yourself is whether or not the model is safe.

Many argue that the system risks becoming an oligopoly; a market structure with a small number of firms where none of them can keep the others from having a significant influence on each other.

To simplify, the market cannot grow because no one can impact the price enough. While most blockchains are against having people in charge, there is a worry that the introduction of validators will lead to Ethereum becoming a centralized platform.

The upside to proof of stake is its solution to energy consumption, as proof of work miners have to sell their coins to pay the power bills to keep things running.

With proof of stake in place, validators can only give power based on the number of coins that they hold.

As a result, proof of stake variations of mining can become more profitable and less costly than their counterparts, but that isn't done without some drawbacks.

This is where the comparison between the two security methods begins, as people endorse proof of work for remaining consistent with the original Bitcoin white paper model.

If proof of stake can successfully work in today's market, then it will prove itself to be a great alternative to the original proof of work method.

If it doesn't live up to its expectations, proof of work will remain the dominant security method used in most blockchains.

Ultimately, it boils down to what the community will accept. Many users in the Ether community are for proof of stake, and praise the ambitious moves that creator Vitalik Buterin has been making since 2013.

There are also others who are against the move, claiming that it would end decentralized trading. However, that end may be approaching faster than originally thought.

Currently, banks and other third parties are banning deposits to crypto exchanges such as Binance and Coinbase due to an excess amount of funds being sent and lost as a result of the crypto frenzy.

Too many find themselves in debt by following ill-advised investment strategies, causing thousands of people everywhere to lose their hard-earned savings overnight.

If banks and other platforms can get a hold of cryptocurrency and turn it into a centralized exchange, proof of stake would be everlastingly dominant in the blockchain network.

Until then, consider it to be an implementation that Ethereum is using to differentiate itself from Bitcoin even more than it already has.

Although it has seen some success in recent years, it might be a while until everyone gets on board with this alternative.

## Conclusion

Proof of stake's success ultimately depends on whether or not the method can be implemented into other cryptocurrencies.

With Ethereum leading the charge, there is a chance that plenty of altcoins will follow the same path, but the question relies on if Bitcoin moves away from proof of work or not.

There is an argument that claims that Bitcoin will never change to proof of stake due to the technical challenges, but many others, such as the founder of the Bitcoin Suisse brokerage, say that the coin will eventually transition to a proof of stake model.

Considering the amount of power that proof of work takes to efficiently mine a cryptocurrency, it seems as if proof of stake will take over soon, and its variable of success ultimately depends on the future of cryptocurrency as a whole.

# Chapter 16: Storing Cryptocurrency

Now that you have a grasp of where crypto comes from, and also how it is a viable investment option, you must now understand where to safely secure your investments.

Online trade is incredibly convenient, but anything that involves the internet landscape as a whole runs a risk of being hacked or stolen.

For this reason, cryptocurrency uses an encryption system known as cryptography which, as discussed in Chapter 2, is a method of encryption that sends the raw message to the sender, an encrypted message to the recipient, and a decrypted message to the destination.

This is done to keep transactions safe and allows traders to comfortably trade their shares without the risk of losing goods in the process.

Although blockchain technology makes it very tough for people to hack into a Bitcoin network, online wallets that act as sources of storage can still be broken into if personal details are lost or retrieved by some means of hacking.

This chapter will serve to show you which method of storage is best for you, as well as will compare the crypto exchange market wallets to the more secure of each form of storage. By having a better understanding of crypto storage, you will be able to keep yourself safe from most forms of security breaches, as well as have a safe place to HODL long-term investments.

You might be asking yourself, "Why do I need to store anything? Isn't the blockchain network incredibly secure?"

Although the blockchain network is very secure, attacks do happen now and then, and when they do, hackers can walk away with thousands to millions' worth of stolen funds.

Exchanges do not compensate their users, so you should choose highly secure options, which will minimize your investment's risk on the platform.

The truth of the matter is that you are likely new to the cryptocurrency system, which makes you the most prone target to take advantage of, and when that hack occurs, you'll be forced to watch your investment dwindle away with no control over it.

To avoid this, you'll need a secure place to lock your investment in, so that no one can manage it or touch it without your permission and command.

## Storage Methods

It is important to note that most forms of crypto storage can transfer crypto between platforms at the user's discretion, in case something goes wrong during the transaction process.

Typically, people use a variety of platforms to track their investments and test out the crypto landscape. This can be anything from multiple exchanges to multiple storage options.

Wallets are cryptocurrencies' preferred method of storage, due to their security and accessibility. As they are called *wallets*, cryptocurrency begins to feel more like a viable form of payment than an online currency you're hoping to make a profit from.

Regardless, there are two major types of storage in cryptocurrency—those being digital wallets and hard wallets—and it is important to differentiate between the two. At the time of writing, there are currently two main crypto wallets available; hot wallets and cold wallets.

## Hot Wallet (Online Wallet)

A hot wallet also referred to as an online wallet, is a storage method that runs on devices capable of connecting to the internet.

Consider it like a checking account; it's easy and available to use at your convenience. You can do whatever you want with the funds, from making additional investments to spending it online, if you wish.

Most hot wallets are built into exchanges like Binance and Coinbase, as the accessibility is convenient that way.

It's the same way that a stock investment app like WealthSimple might work; you can see your balance and your gains as you wish, while also having the option of withdrawing, selling, or exchanging your funds.

Its convenience is one of its biggest advantages, and the ability to access at will makes crypto investing incredibly mobile.

Most hot wallets are available as software applications on mobile phones and laptops, so as long as you have an internet connection of some sort, you'll be able to check and manage everything whenever you wish.

Although this may sound like the best option available, it does have its flaws; primarily, security is one of the biggest concerns.

Crypto exchanges are very secure, but the amount of security you get relies on you as a crypto investor.

If your account has an easy-to-guess password, no 2FA authentication, or you have disabled email notifications regarding unwarranted log-ins, you'll find yourself prone and vulnerable to hacks and data breaches.

This is what you want to avoid, and it is your responsibility as an online trader to make sure that your account is secure by choosing the best options available.

### Cold Wallet (Hardware Wallets)

As the name might suggest, cold wallets are opposite to hot wallets, meaning that they don't require internet connections.

Cold wallets, also referred to as hardware wallets, are pieces of hardware that store cryptocurrency on a drive.

This eliminates the risk of security breaches, so long as you maintain access to your drive.

The wallet stores the user's online address and private key and comes with software that works parallel to hot wallets.

In this way, the portfolios can be viewed without putting a private key at risk.

Hard wallets do not correlate with the exchange market, other than applying the fluctuation of price to ensure that an investment is actually placed.

Instead, they serve as a security measure; a storage space that keeps your crypto safe from any kind of exposure, such as hacks or data breaches.

If you're going to be a long-term investor, this option is very viable, as the online world continues to suffer from daily exposure to online hacks, as well as recently seeing an increase of fraudulent miners and fraudulent investors looking to make a quick buck off of the misfortunate.

This is not to say that digital wallets and exchanges are not secure—just that hard wallets tend to do a better job of ensuring security.

Most hardware wallets are designed as USB devices, which have serious advantages over soft wallets.

For example, hardware wallets aren't affected by viruses because the private keys used never come in contact with a network or other vulnerable software.

Because they require a computer to access and not an internet connection, any malicious changes must be done manually.

That means that a thief would first have to steal your USB drive, then guess the password, then go through the encryption, and only then would they have access to your portfolio.

What's even better is that these devices are open source, meaning that there's likely a community on GitHub developing additional software to increase security.

With a community backing the storage option instead of a company, this might be the most enticing option for you as an investor.

Both forms of storage can also transfer crypto between each other at the user's discretion, in case something goes awry. Typically, people use a wide variety of platforms to track their investments and test out the crypto landscape.

The downside to hardware wallets is the setup, primarily because it may take a bit of knowledge to get them to work.

For larger investments, this storage option is likely the way to go in terms of security.

## Not My Keys, Not My Problem

We touched on hot wallets and their connections to exchanges, but it is important to expand that concept to the most of its plausible understanding.

If something were to happen to your account, such as a malicious attack on the network, where you suffer a loss as a result, **you will not be compensated**.

Cryptocurrency exchanges do not offer any form of insurance, so safe storage is crucial when working through a trade.

The phrase *not my keys, not my problem* specifically refers to such a concept, which is why it isn't wise to keep a large amount of money in either a hot wallet or an exchange account.

It is better to deposit those funds into a cold wallet so that only you can access them.

Online trading is one of the biggest innovations of the modern era; however, anything online can be hacked or broken into at the click of a button.

Ensure your privacy by spreading out your portfolio, and only keep what you're willing to spend (at the moment) in a hot wallet.

**Overview**

When comparing storage options, it's best to think of them all as checking, savings, and investing accounts.

A hot wallet would be a checking account, meaning that you can spend whatever is in there with no major setback to your portfolio.

Hot wallets can also be investing accounts if you work through an exchange, with your portfolio gains and losses available at any moment if you wish to trade more.

Cold wallets can be considered to be your savings accounts, and you should leave large sums of money in there to ensure you're getting the most out of that investment.

In general, try to layout your funds as you would your usual investments, and design a system that works best for yourself.

Cryptocurrency works because it is unique to the individual, so it's best to find an option that works best for you.

Most traders will spread their investments out on multiple platforms, while others will stick to only one.

Examine your available options, and choose the best storage methods as appropriate.

## Chapter 17: Cryptocurrency and the Tax Man

Investing in cryptocurrency, as proven by previous points shown, can be incredibly profitable.

However, it is a currency after all, and the IRS is going to tax you on your profits. You'll need to understand how taxes are assessed, as well as how to evaluate how much you owe.

In addition, you will also need to prepare for tax payments, as cryptocurrency is treated as a capital asset, which is taxed when sold for profit.

In order to maximize your profits as much as you can, you must prepare yourself for those taxes and the fees that come along with them.

The decision to tax crypto was seen as a major setback for investors and many people worried that the government may have plans to make the platforms into centralized exchanges.

At the time of writing, banks have banned transactions to major exchanges, which is also a concern for investors.

Although it may have been a pragmatic move by the IRS, cryptocurrency will continue to be a taxable entity for the foreseeable future.

Due to these factors, this chapter will touch on assessing your tax strategy, evaluating how much you will have to pay, and what you should do when taxes are due.

It may seem complicated, but its basic principles share a lot in common with the stock market. Take your time and follow at your own pace so that you can understand the concepts coming your way.

**How Are Taxes Assessed?**

Crypto has been taxable since 2014 when the IRS ruled it as a capital asset rather than legal tender.

As such, crypto owners are susceptible to taxes and, as previously stated, are taxed when sold for profit. Those taxes are evaluated based on profits gained.

For example, if your US$20 investment rises to US$200 in value, you'll owe taxes on the $180 profit that you made from your investment.

The same ideology is used with stocks and bonds, and they are typically assessed similarly.

The reason why crypto is taxable today is that it is seen as an investment, and even though there is no central party overlooking the system, the IRS is legally obligated to tax a percentage of your investments.

When depositing your profits into your bank account, for example, that is taxed as additional income.

Cryptocurrency has trading volumes with millions of dollars in valuation, and the IRS was previously missing out on that source of revenue.

As such, cryptocurrency will continue to be taxed, as long as it is seen as a viable investment option.

There is an upside to tax assessments, as you only get taxed on the profit you make from selling your investment.

If you sell at a loss or lose your investment entirely, you don't have to pay any taxes at all on those amounts.

The IRS recognizes cryptocurrency as a volatile trade and understands that taxes shouldn't be assessed on a loss.

For example, if you invested in Bitcoin at US$10,000 and sold it for US$13,000, you would be taxed on a gain of US$3,000.

However, if you sell at US$7,000 instead, you'll owe nothing in taxes for the sale, and a part or all of the US$3,000 that would have otherwise been assessed could be used toward other investment opportunities.

From here, all you need to understand is how to assess how much you owe in taxes.

**How Much Do I Owe?**

The amount you owe in tax is based upon two factors; your annual income, and how long you've held your investment.

Holding your investment for less than a year before selling it for a profit would be known as short-term capital gains, which are taxed at your usual income rate.

However, if you instead held your investment for more than a year, your profits would be considered to be long-term capital gains, which are taxed at a lower rate and are also determined by your annual income. If you earned cryptocurrency by mining or from a promotion for a good or service, you will be taxed on the entire value of the crypto on the day you received it.

In general, the amount you owe in taxes all depends on how you obtained the cryptocurrency, which can be any of the following:

- Mining rewards

The rewards you gain from mining cryptocurrency are taxable, and you'll likely be taxed based on the entire value of the reward.

- Crypto gifts

Gaining crypto through a promotion, gift, or airdrop, is considered to be taxable income, meaning that it will be added to your total income for the year.

- Method of payment

If someone paid you for services with cryptocurrency, the entire payment amount counts as taxable income.

This is the same method used with legal tender, however, the customer may also incur tax if the value of the crypto provides them with more than they paid for.

- Selling for gains

As previously stated, selling your crypto investment for gains works the same as it would with stocks. You will owe tax depending on the number of gains you received.

- Exchanging between other users and coins

Things are a bit different when exchanging one cryptocurrency for another. You'll owe tax on any gains you earn in the transaction, which is done to even out the amount you're exchanging.

For example, if you convert US$400 worth of Bitcoin into US$1,000 of Ethereum, you'll owe tax on the US$600 to the IRS.

Although you're just exchanging one coin for another, the value is assessed to keep you at your initial investment. This is why many users follow the HODL strategy and spread their investments out accordingly.

Additionally, if you hold crypto from these activities, they can be turned into short- or long-term capital gains, which is a better option if you plan to invest the rewards into something worth more than their current value.

**Minimizing Your Taxes**
The prospect of losing additional gains to the taxman can be frustrating. Fortunately, there are a few steps that you can take to minimize your taxes, such as:

1. Turning short-term gains into long-term gains

Capital gains rates all depend on how long you have owned the cryptocurrency.

If you wish to lower your taxes, it is advisable to hold your gains for more than one year, to turn your short-term gains into long-term gains.

It will require patience and perseverance, and with that, you'll likely end up paying a reduced tax rate on the capital gains.

For example, say an investor earns US$5,000 in capital gains thanks to cryptocurrency investing.

If that gain is considered to be short-term, then that extra money is considered to be additional income and is taxed accordingly, even after claiming the standard deductions.

However, if the gain is considered to be long-term, then that crypto investment gain of US$5,000 is only taxable at 15%, allowing you to keep more of your investment and lower your taxes as a result.

2. Offsetting gains with losses

You should also consider offsetting your capital gains with your capital losses, which works by subtracting the losses on your crypto assets that you sold during the year's timespan from taxable gains on crypto or other investments that have risen in value.

However, there are limitations to this strategy, as when you realize investment losses, you need to offset any losses of the same type.

Short-term losses first reduce short-term gains, and vice versa for long-term gains. If you have any net losses of either type, they can be used to offset any capital gains.

That means that even short-term losses can be applied to any long-term capital gains, so long as they remain as investment gains at that time.

If there are any losses available after offsetting, you can use them to lower your normal annual income.

Sadly, however, that is limited to US$3,000 of capital losses that can be applied in one year. The remaining balance would then be applied to the next year, which offsets future gains and lowers annual income by up to US$3,000.

3.  Sell in a low-income year

Timing is important in cryptocurrency, and the same can be said for your taxes. By selling in a low-income year, you can reduce your taxes by a decent margin.

As stated previously, any capital gains are added to your taxes as additional income, so by selling in a low-income year, you set yourself up to be in a lower tax bracket than you normally would be.

As such, you'll experience a lower tax rate. This is best if you are currently considering retirement, as you naturally wouldn't have any ordinary income coming your way.

In fact, if this is the case, your entire tax bracket could simply be a variable of your short-term capital gains.

Additionally, if you choose to retire early and have enough cash to fund your daily life expenses (until you touch your retirement funds), you'll likely have little to no income for the year.

Selling your capital gains now would lock you in for the long term, and you might find yourself paying a 0% tax rate.

Consider your current situation as a variable in this case, and if a low-income year is on its way, sell your assets and lower your tax rate as a result.

4. Reduce your taxable income

In addition to selling your profits during a low-income year, your crypto taxes can be minimized if you reduce your actual taxable income.

This is a common true tax minimization strategy, which works by sourcing the tax code for tax deductions and credits that help to reduce your total taxable income.

This can be anything from taking care of medical problems, contributing to an IRA or 401K plan, putting money in a health savings account, or donating your profits to charity.

There are many options besides these, so consider asking a tax professional to help you to uncover other tax breaks that apply to you.

After all, the goal is to keep as much of your investment gains for yourself, so hiring the extra help may pay off in the long run.

5. Investing in a retirement account

Another method that crypto investors use to minimize their crypto tax bill is investing their profits in a tax-deferred or tax-free Self-Directed Individual Retirement Account, (SDIRA).

In this way, your taxes can only be incurred when you withdraw out of this account, which allows you to wait for a low-income year.

Additionally, it also works as a retirement account, and your taxes can be lowered if you're currently retired and expect a higher tax rate as a result of your withdrawn funds.

6. Gifting to a family member

This method is dependent on your goals for crypto investing, and if you wish to use your wealth for another purpose, you may want to consider another method of lowering your taxes.

Otherwise, another method of lowering taxes involves gifting assets to family members.

This works because the IRS ultimately allows you to give up to US$15,000 per year without any tax consequences.

That rate is applied per person, meaning that you can give two people US$15,000 each with no conceivable tax incurred.

Additionally, if the recipient is at a low enough income, they will incur little to no tax in their tax bracket as well.

This strategy is entirely dependent on your investment plans, however, and if you wish to transfer your profits at all, you need to discuss the matter with a professional such as an estate planner to ensure that your plans will meet your overall needs.

## 7.  Donating to charity

On May 12, 2021, Ethereum creator Vitalik Buterin donated about US$1 Billion worth of meme-coins, such as DOGE, to several non-profit organizations in India so that they could effectively combat the COVID-19 pandemic.

Although this was widely seen as a move of generosity, it was also likely a move that lowered the creator's taxes by a wide margin.

Similar to gifting assets to a family member, the strategy incurs no capital gains tax, and may also trigger a significant tax reduction that you may be able to claim on your tax return.

Whenever you donate an asset, you can claim the fair market value of that asset at the time of donation as a tax reduction on your income.

For example, if you donate US$50,000 worth of Bitcoin to charity, you may be able to write it off as a charitable deduction.

Additionally, if the charity qualifies itself as tax-exempt, no tax will be incurred on any capital gains when it sells the donation later.

Overall, if you can afford to send some profits to charity, it can benefit your taxable income in the long run.

## 8. Moving to a state with no income tax

If your plans for the future involve moving states, then this option may work for you.

State-level income taxes are a part of most people's lives, as the state typically has an interest in everyone's investment gains.

However, many tax-friendly states offer low or no income taxes, meaning that you would not owe much in the way of tax to the state's treasury.

You may find yourself paying tax at the federal level, but the rates are still low enough to warrant moving states, and you would keep a large portion of your investment.

## 9. Bequeathing it from your estate

The final strategy for minimizing crypto taxes here is to bequeath your crypto assets as a part of your estate.

When you pass away, the investment will see an increase to its fair market value at your time of death.

In this way, your family heirs (or whoever you have chosen as a beneficiary) will not incur tax on their original basis, which may lower the total tax incurred by a significant margin.

The issue here is the volatility in cryptocurrency, as prices can spike high or low at any given moment.

If those crypto assets rise higher than their fair market value, the tax will be applied, but won't be as high as it would have been, thanks to your heirs receiving the coins on a stepped-up basis.

Although this won't help your tax bracket by a wide margin, if your financial plans are to set your heirs up for fortune after you're gone, then this option is worth considering for all involved in the process.

### Overview

At the end of the day, the IRS is always going to take some dividend from any investment that you profit from.

Every investor, in one way or another, is a taxpayer, meaning that everyone is required to report capital gains on their tax returns.

This includes cryptocurrency, and the IRS continuously tracks those profits as the exchange expands and evolves.

You shouldn't try to avoid incurring tax with every transaction, as that can land you in some serious legal trouble as well.

Instead, take steps to lower your taxes by managing your investments according to your gains. In that way, in a normal market, you won't experience as much tax as you initially would in a typical investment scenario.

If the market is currently experiencing a bull run, tax payments will likely be at their highest with everyone selling their profits at a consistent rate.

This isn't to say that the tax rate changes depending on the market; it actually depends on a ratio between your total annual income and the gains from your investments.

Due to the bull run, you'll likely be selling your investments at the peak of their valuation, which is great for your bank account, but bad for your taxes.

Be sure to budget accordingly and leave money aside to pay them off, as you won't want to pay taxes out of pocket.

It's best recommended that you pay your crypto taxes with the profits you have available, and then use the remaining profits to reinvest at another time.

Overall, it's completely up to you to manage your investments, and taxes should never be an afterthought in the investment process.

## Chapter 18: Tracking the Money

You've chosen an exchange, chosen crypto to invest in, put down a deposit, and secure your investment in storage that best suits your needs.

All you need to do now is find a way to track your investment to stay up to date with your portfolio, so a portfolio tracker is exactly what you need.

With these tools at your disposal, you'll be able to manage and track your crypto investments at the touch of your fingertips, allowing you to make any changes whenever you want to.

Before you dive into the available options, we should first elaborate on what crypto portfolio trackers are, and how they can help you in the long run

### Crypto Portfolio Trackers

The cryptocurrency market was a lot simpler when Bitcoin was the only thing people were buying; however, today's market consists of thousands upon thousands of crypto options for investment purposes.

As such, there are plenty of opportunities in which to invest and make something from your deposit.

People would typically split their investments up through different exchange apps and would make changes to each exchange's hot wallet balance accordingly.

This became problematic, as it can be hard to manage the numbers when fumbling through so many apps. This is where portfolio trackers come into play.

The need to have accounts at multiple exchanges made it difficult to track the total profits and losses for the day, which is why portfolio trackers were implemented for the cryptocurrency trading scene.

A portfolio tracker allows a user to track all of their investments on a single app. Some apps even use API, meaning that the entire process of tracking the portfolio's value is automated.

As an investor's portfolio can be tracked and simplified in one app, investors no longer have to jump between multiple exchanges to view their investments.

They can look at everything as a whole, and make changes according to the total value that they see. So, which options are best for you, and how do you know which one to choose?

## Best Available Options

Listed below are a few portfolio trackers that have been tested by users all over the world, which include the following:

## Blockfolio

Blockfolio is considered by many to be the best option for investors looking for a portfolio tracker.

This is due to its superior design traits, as well as a solid user experience, especially when it comes to backing up the application.

Blockfolio tracks nearly every crypto asset (10,000 or more) and has a list of exchange connections that can be used for other trading purposes.

At the time of writing, there are 15 exchanges available on the Blockfolio app.

The app is based around a project intelligence tool known as Signal, which combines news and other helpful data with your investments and portfolio.

With this, you can understand the everyday changes that are surrounding your investment, and what could potentially be affecting it.

The app also allows you to set up price alerts for any coin of choice, such as Bitcoin or Ethereum, so you can know when a coin's price is finally at your preferred buying point.

Considering that it has near-perfect reviews on the Apple Store and that the app is completely free to use, there aren't many options as good as this one when it comes to portfolio tracking.

## Kubera

The idea of a portfolio tracker is likely enticing, and you may be wondering if there's an option to track other investments as well.

Trackers like Mint and Personal Capital can do that, but they don't track cryptocurrency, and we want to avoid jumping through multiple apps and websites if possible.

The goal is simple accessibility, so everything changed when Kubera partnered with Zabo to make that happen. Kubera not only tracks crypto investments, but it also tracks other financial assets as well.

By letting you connect all your financial accounts in one place, tracking is as easy as ever. It has a simple and clean design, and Kubera prides itself on keeping data away from third parties.

It supports a wide range of crypto accounts, including all the top-tier exchanges, and it also has a helpful estate management system, which allows you to send your info to a beneficiary if something bad happens to you.

Although it costs $12 per month (or $120 per year) and is only available on the web, Kubera is great for keeping everything in one place.

## Delta

For pure crypto trackers, Delta emerges as another viable option. After being acquired by eToro, another platform with 13 million users, the Delta app works to track cryptocurrency investments with the best accuracy possible.

Additionally, at the time of writing, a Delta 2.0 is in the works to compete with Kubera, as the company wishes to track both crypto and financial assets.

Delta is also competitive with Blockfolio, and for good reason.

Both have a strong list of exchange and wallet connections, and Delta has its own project intelligence tool known as Delta Direct, which also gives news and updates about your favorite coins.

Delta also allows users to set up price alerts, just like Blockfolio and is free to use for a set of basic features.

Its drawback is exactly that, however, as to unlock the full list of features, such as multi-device syncing and unlimited exchange connections, you'll have to pay about $60 per year.

It's also mobile-only, which may be a drawback for some, but for a basic option that looks visually better than Blockfolio, Delta is a great crypto portfolio tracker.

**Lunch Money**

Lunch Money is based around their tagline *Delightfully simple budgeting* and is currently partnered with Zabo, the same company that partnered with Kubera.

The app has a unique and fun design and can track all financial accounts, just like Kubera.

It also has budgeting tools to help with investments, such as a rules engine that automatically tags and categorizes transactions using CSV imports or API implications.

Their only drawbacks are the same as others; the app is web-based only and charges a monthly fee of about $7 per month if paid annually.

Regardless, considering the entire app was developed by one person, Lunch Money receives plenty of updates to keep itself running efficiently.

## CoinStats

CoinStats is one of the few trackers that are available on almost every platform and it prides itself on being a cross-platform product.

It is currently available on iOS, Android, Mac desktops, iWatch, and as a Google Chrome extension. It also has a wide selection of crypto account connections, and they routinely push out new features to keep things fresh and up to date.

It's free to get started, but that's just for the basic features. CoinStats is not free past a number of connections and has a limited upload history.

In order to get unlimited connections, you'll need to pay either $3.50 per month for the Pro version or about $14 per month for the Premium version.

## Zerion

Zerion is one of the only DeFi portfolio trackers available that was founded in 2016 as a way to track Ethereum and other applications early on in the DeFi evolution.

Most DeFi apps are considered to be clunky and hard to use, but Zerion is an exception, winning awards for the best UX in 2019.

It covers a wide variety of DeFi specification functions, and constantly adds new integrations to stay up to date with

DeFi's current evolution. Zerion is also one of the only portfolio trackers that allows you to trade assets, borrow money, or invest in other DeFi products from the app itself.

Considering that it's free to use, it's an all-in-one deal for DeFi investors.

The downside is that you can only track Ethereum and DeFi assets right now, so it isn't useful for a total crypto evaluation.

However, if your bet is with Ethereum and the DeFi community, then consider Zerion as the best DeFi portfolio tracker available.

## What Should I Choose?

Portfolio trackers are entirely dependent on the user's needs, as tracking your investment is an important part of the investing process.

There are more options available than the ones listed here, so be sure to research outside of the text provided, and find something that is comfortable for your needs and your investments.

If one of the options here entices you enough, give it a try, and remember that portfolio trackers are not limited to just cryptocurrency.

Tracking your other financial assets is just as important, and you should find an option that is as diverse and accessible as possible for all of your investments.

## Overview

On May 25, 2021, CNBC released an article about Cooper Turley who, at 25, became a millionaire after investing in Bitcoin and Ethereum at an early stage.

He held those investments for four years until the valuation was right to sell, and now has the funds to set himself and his family up for the rest of their lives.

I, myself, have personally used all of the tactics contained in this guide to help me get to where I am today with my own investments, from starting in 2011 with mining rigs to paying for homes using the profit I made from crypto investing.

Cryptocurrency can be a complicated, convoluted, and frustrating subject to look into and research for investment purposes.

However, with the right guidance and information, crypto investments can be made at will and can see immense valuation within a few years of investing.

Sure, some situations lead to profits overnight, but that's more about being in the right place at the right time than it is about investment strategies.

Now that you've reached the end of this guide, you can get started with investing the second you close the cover.

Some of the steps you should take should include the following:

- Research a coin you wish to invest in.
- Find a reliable exchange where you can place a deposit.
- Separate your trading shares and your investment shares into different storage wallets.
- Check your investments periodically to confirm the valuation.

Once you've done that, you're practically set. Considering that you have all the tools at your disposal, there is no time like the present for you to go out and use them.

However, it is important to reiterate a main piece of information: cryptocurrency is an incredibly volatile trade.

Only invest what you can afford to lose, and be sure to budget yourself accordingly. Overall, you're now prepared to invest in cryptocurrency, so go ahead and get started.

If you enjoyed this guide or found it helpful in any way at all, please take two minutes of your time to review it on Amazon and share what you think with other reviewers on the site.

# References

Adams, R. (2021, May 20). *9 ways to cut crypto taxes down to the bone.* https://www.kiplinger.com/taxes /capital-gains-tax/602825/ways- to-cut-crypto-taxes-down-to-the- bone.

Boundless. (n.d.). *Boundless Statistics.* Lumen. https://courses.lumenlearning.co m/boundless- statistics/chapter/the-law-of- averages/.

CryptoVantage. (2021, April 9). *Reviews of the best crypto portfolio trackers for 2021.* CryptoVantage. https://www.cryptovantage.com/ best-crypto-portfolio-trackers/.

*Decentralized finance (DeFi).* ethereum.org. (n.d.). https://ethereum.org/en/defi/#d efi-vs-tradfi.

Frankenfield, J. (2021, June 24). *Hard fork (Blockchain) definition.* Investopedia. https://www.investopedia.com/terms/h/hard-fork.asp.

Frankenfield, J. (2021, May 19). *Proof of stake (PoS).* Investopedia. https://www.investopedia.com/terms/p/proof-stake-pos.asp.

Frankenfield, J. (2021, May 19). *Soft fork definition.* Investopedia. https://www.investopedia.com/terms/s/soft-fork.asp.

Frankenfield, J. (2021, May 19). *What is zk-SNARK?* Investopedia. https://www.investopedia.com/terms/z/zksnark.asp.

Futurism. (2017, June 28). *Blockchain and renewable energy are utterly disrupting society as we know it.* Futurism. https://futurism.com/blockchain-and-renewable-energy-are-utterly-disrupting-society-as-we-know-it.

Hertig, A. (2020, December 22). *What is proof-of-work?* CoinDesk. https://www.coindesk.com/what -is-proof-of-work.

*The history of Bitcoin: How did Bitcoin become so popular?* Shrimpy Academy. (n.d.). https://academy.shrimpy.io/post /the-history-of-bitcoin-how-did-bitcoin-become-so-popular.

*Home.* IOTA. (n.d.). https://www.iota.org/.

Hong, E. (2021, July 14). *How does Bitcoin mining work?* Investopedia. https://www.investopedia.com/t ech/how-does-bitcoin-mining-work/.

*If you bought 1 Dogecoin 5 years ago, here's how much you'd have today.* The Motley Fool. (2021, June 25). https://www.fool.com/the-ascent/buying-stocks/articles/if-you-bought-1-dogecoin-5-years-ago-heres-how-much-youd-have-today/.

Locke, T. (2021, May 24). *This 25-year-old says he's a millionaire after investing early in Ether and Bitcoin.* CNBC. https://www.cnbc.com/2021/05/21/how-crypto-investor-bought-btc-eth-early-used-defi.html.

Marr, B. (2018, March 20). *Blockchain: A very short history Of Ethereum everyone should read.* Forbes. https://www.forbes.com/sites/bernardmarr/2018/02/02/blockchain-a-very-short-history-of-ethereum-everyone-should-read/?sh=6e8d83bf1e89.

Millenaar, J. (n.d.). *The case for a unified identity.* IOTA. https://files.iota.org/comms/IOTA_The_Case_for_a_Unified_Identity.pdf.

Nakamoto, S. (2011). *Bitcoin white paper.* Bitcoin.org. https://bitcoin.org/bitcoin.pdf.

*Peer-to-Peer Electronic cash*. Bitcoin Cash. (n.d.). https://bitcoincash.org/.

*Possible economic consequences of digital cash*. (n.d.). https://web.archive.org/web/20160103053453/http://www.isoc.org/inet96/proceedings/b1/b1_1.htm#:~:text=On%20the%20mother%20and%2C%20it,overshadows%20 these%20 benefits%20and%20problems.

Rodeck, D. (2021, May 27). *How is cryptocurrency taxed?* Forbes. https://www.forbes.com/advisor/investing/what-are-cryptocurrency-taxes/.

Singh, M. (2021, May 12). *Ethereum creator donates $1 billion worth of meme coins to India*. TechCrunch. https://techcrunch.com/2021/05/12/vitalik-buterin-donates-1-billion-worth-of-meme-coins-to-india-covid-relief-fund/.

10 easy ways to decide which cryptocurrency to invest in! (2021, April 17). https://kingpassive.com/which-cryptocurrency-to-invest-in/.

Treece, A. (2021, January 15). *7 Best crypto portfolio trackers for 2021 (Tried & Tested)*. Zabo's Blog. https://zabo.com/blog/best-crypto-portfolio-tracker/.

*What is Blockchain technology? How does it work?: Built in*. What is Blockchain technology? How does it work? | Built In. (n.d.). https://builtin.com/blockchain.

*Why the "buy and hold" strategy works best for Bitcoin trading*. RSS. (n.d.). https://www.youhodler.com/blog/hodl-bitcoin.

Wikimedia Foundation. (2021, July 19). *Dogecoin*. Wikipedia. https://en.wikipedia.org/wiki/Dogecoin.

*The world's most accessible, no-limit betting platform.* Augur. (n.d.). https://augur.net/.

# Back Cover

## The Baby Boomer's Guide to Cryptocurrency

The Baby Boomer's Guide to Cryptocurrency... How to buy, sell, trade, mine, and make cryptocurrency part of your portfolio

By C.B. McGee

**Discover how baby boomers like you can get their portfolios booming with crypto, even with zero experience.**

Cryptocurrencies are evolving by the day, and more people are profiting from it while you're stuck figuring out how they're doing it.

It can be frustrating, but the good news is that with the right action-based guide and mindset, you'll soon be on the path to achieving your financial goals.

The first step to becoming successful in the world of crypto is having the insight and understanding that other wealthy investors have—and using it to take constructive action.

C.B. McGee has all the answers you're looking for, and you'll benefit from his methods for investing in cryptocurrency.

In *The Baby Boomer's Guide to Cryptocurrency*, here is just a fraction of what you will discover:

A comprehensive guide to the world of cryptocurrencies so you can keep up with all the latest trends

How people are making millions of dollars from a crypto that started off as a joke

The most powerful investment strategies so you can always get the most bang for your buck

The latest research in crypto mining and how to know if it's worth investing your time and money

A goldmine of crypto terminology that's easy to understand and even teach to others

Professional secrets on buying, selling, and investing crypto, so it's safe and profitable